THE BACKPACKER'S COOKBOOK

Rita van Dyk

Copyright © 1992 Rita van Dyk

All rights reserved. No part of this publication may be
reproduced or transmitted in any form or by any means
without prior written permission from the publisher

ISBN 0 620 16868 4

First edition, first impression 1992
Published by the author

Cover photograph by Dewald Reiners
Cover design by Loretta Steyn
Set in Times Roman
Printed and bound by CTP Book Printers, Cape Town

Trade enquiries: Rita van Dyk
       P O Box 23874
       Innesdale
       0031

Whilst every effort was made to obtain permission
for copyright, some information and recipes were
obtained from friends and other hikers and the
original source is therefore unknown. The author would
be grateful to rectify this in any subsequent edition of
the publication.

The information on haybox cooking on page 22 is adapted from THE SOUTH
AFRICAN BACKPACKER by Helmke Hennig, with kind permission from
the author

BK3169

ACKNOWLEDGEMENTS

This book would not have been possible without the help of a lot of people: Gert Basson, Kobie Gouws and Hettie Scholtz for teaching me the mechanics of publishing; friends and co-hikers for sharing with me their favourite recipes; my husband Johan for his unwavering support; Bedelia Basson for encouragement; Wolfgang Fedder for technical advice; Catherine Murray, Dewald Reiners, Loretta Steyn and Geoff Horne for fast and professional services.

CONTENTS

Introduction	13
Useful Conversions	15
Cutlery and Cooking Equipment	17
Tips for Packing Food	18
Nutrition	19
Three-day menu for a group of three	20
How to Cook Dehydrated Vegetables	21
Haybox Cooking	22
Hassle-free Instant Meals	24
Breakfast	24
Lunch	25
Dinner	25
Desserts	26
Snacks	27
Cereals and Porridge	29
Basic Granola	29
Crunchy Breakfast Mix	29
Crunchy Granola	30
Fruit and Nut Muesli	31
Muesli Base	31
Muesli I	32
Muesli II	32
Oatmeal Porridge	33
Bread and Rusks	34
Bran Rusks	34
Chapatis	34
Garlic Bread	35
Indian Coconut Bread	35
Nutty Yoghurt Bread	36
Quick Bread Mix	36
Stick Bread	37
Trail Bread	38

Yoghurt Bran Bread	38
Spreads and Pâtés	40
Biltong Pâté I	40
Biltong Pâté II	40
Cheese Spread	41
Energy Smear	41
Fig Sandwich Spread	41
Green Bean and Walnut Pâté	42
Peanut Butter	42
Peanut Butter Filling	42
Peanut Butter and Fruit Spread	43
Nuts and Seeds	44
Candied Orange Pecans	44
Curried Nuts	44
Mexican Nuts	45
Roasted Soya Beans	45
Seed Snacks	46
Spicy Nuts I	46
Spicy Nuts II	47
Sugar and Spice Nuts	47
Tangy Sunflower Seeds	48
Fruit Nibbles	49
Apple Snack	49
Apricotlets	49
Apricot Jujubes	50
Apricot Sweets	50
Blind Dates	51
Filled Fruit Rolls	51
Fruit Balls	52
Fruit Rolls	52
Golden Crunch Balls	53
Mixed Fruit Snack	53
Orange Peel in Syrup	54
Peanut Butter and Banana Leather	55
Sesame Fruit Balls	55
Stuffed Prunes	55

Surprise Prunes	56
Energy Bars and Sweet Nibbles	57
Almond Squares	57
Apricot Coconut Bars	57
Brazil Nut Bars	58
Chewy Hazelnut Bars	58
Crispy Date Bars	59
Date Pinwheels	59
Date Squares	60
Energy Bars	61
Fig Fudge	61
Fruit and Nut Bars	62
Fruit Bars	62
Fruit Crunchies	63
Knapsack Cookies	63
Muesli Bars	64
Nut Squares	65
PB Bars	65
Peanut Brittle	66
Peanut Butter Bars	66
Peanut Butter Fudge	67
Peanut Butter and Granola Bars	67
Pear-lemon Squares	68
Quick Fruit Bars	69
Seed Biscuits	70
Sesame Confection	70
Sesame Seed Biscuits	71
Shortbread	71
Savoury Nibbles	72
Biltong Fingers	72
Herbed Wholewheat Straws	72
Nibbler's Treat	72
Sesame Seed Nibbles	73
Wheat Germ Sticks	73
Soup and Dumplings	74
Cheese and Rice Soup	74

Cream of Sweetcorn Soup	75
Homemade Dry Soup Mix	75
Parsley Scone Dumplings	76

Salads

Bean Sprouts	77
Rice and Green Pepper Salad	77
Salad of India	77
Tuna Salad	78

Savoury Sauces

Easy Barbecue Sauce	79
Green Sauce for Pasta	79

Pasta

Bacon and Noodles	80
Chilli Fusilli	81
Chinese Noodles with Napoli Sauce	82
Curry Noodles	82
Funghi Fusilli	83
Green Ribbon Pasta with Tuna Sauce	83
Lasagne	84
Macaroni Cheese	84
Noodles with Walnut Sauce	85
Prawn Pasta	86
Red Beans and Pasta	86
Spaghetti Bolognaise	87
Summer Party Pasta	87
Tagliatelle with Salami and Cheese	88
Tortellini in Cream	88
Trail Spaghetti Dinner	89
Tuna Curry Noodles	89
Tuna Spirals	90
Warm Spaghetti Salad	90

Vegetables

Asparagus	91
Cabbage in Cheese Sauce	91
Carrots and Potatoes	91
Carrots in White Sauce	91

Cheesy Baked Potatoes	92
Green Beans in Mushroom Sauce	92
Mint-glazed Carrots with Peas	92
Mushrooms	93
Potato Nests	93
Rice Patties	93
Risotto	94
Sautéed Sprouts	94
Stewed Cabbage	95
Sweet Potatoes	95
Sweet Potatoes in Foil	95
Sweet Potatoes with Marshmallows	95
Tasty Instant Potatoes	96
Other Main Meals	**97**
Baked Potatoes with Shrimps or Mussels	97
Biltong Potjie	97
Cheese Fondue	98
Chicken à La King	98
Cooked-in-the-pan Pizza Margherita	99
Curried Salmon	100
Hamburger Patties	100
Kipper Pie	101
Lentil Curry	101
Malay Bobotie	102
Meal-in-one	102
Savoury Mince	103
Shepherd's Pie	103
Spiced Black-eyed Beans	104
Trail Casserole	105
Vegetarian Bobotie	105
Desserts	**107**
Apple and Date Charlotte	107
Baked Stuffed Apples	107
Caramelled Apples	108
Caramel Popcorn	108
Caramel Sauce	109

Cardinal Peaches	109
Chocolate Fondue I	110
Chocolate Fondue II	110
Chocolate-stuffed Bananas	111
Cornflake Flan	111
Custard	112
Date Filling for Flan	112
Fried Apple Rings	112
Honey and Almond Fondue	113
Mock Cream Sauce	113
Noodle and Prune Bake	114
Orange Cream	114
Oranges in Foil	115
Pears in Red Wine	115
Prune Stew	115
Simple Baked Apples	116
Spiced Apples with Honey	116
Trifle	117
Drinks	118
Banana Milk Shake	118
Brown Russian	118
Chocolate Soldier	119
Cocoa	119
Ginger Tea	119
Harry's Cape Velvet	120
Hot Punch	120
Hot Semolina Drink	121
Hot Spiced Orange Juice	121
Mozart Coffee	121
Peanut Milk	122

INTRODUCTION

Food is very much a personal thing: what one person considers delicious, another might find unacceptable; what one person might consider too much trouble to prepare, another might find worth the effort; some backpackers will carry heavy tins to avoid eating dehydrated food while for others weight will be the determining factor in deciding what to eat.

This book endeavours to cater for all tastes and preferences. But in the end good, common sense must prevail. It is senseless to carry heavy items such as tins and food containing water on a long wilderness trail. On a strenuous trail the main consideration for selecting food should be that it must weigh as little as possible, while still containing the right nutritional value. On the other hand, it is unnecessary to take dehydrated food on a short, easy hike when fresh food will keep well. The size of the hiking group is also a determining factor in selecting food, as the items could be divided amongst the group and the weight per person is therefore reduced.

Always plan a menu in advance of the hike and test the recipes at home to make sure you like them. Also test the size of the portions (these will naturally differ from person to person, but must almost always be bigger than usual on a hike). Prepare ingredients at home where necessary, such as grating cheese or chopping food in a food processor. Lastly, make sure your pot or pan is big enough for the dishes you intend to prepare. Reduce or increase the ingredients to suit the size of your group.

Some of the recipes in the book take time to prepare and you might not feel like going to a lot of trouble when you're tired. Once again, be sensible. Buy prepacked foods or prepare some of the easier dishes on a tough hike. However, if you know you're going to have a birthday party, or if you are taking turns to cook, it will be a special treat to eat pizza or lasagne for dinner!

In planning your menu, keep in mind that you should not carry more than 1 kg of food per person per day. If you find your food is too heavy, substitute tins and fresh foodstuff with dehydrated items.

Unless you are so fixed in your ways that you pack the same food for every hike, a lot of preparation goes into planning a creative, delicious menu. Camping stores seldom stock a wide variety of food and a visit to a supermarket is usually necessary to complete your purchases. Be open-minded and imaginative and look for new products that can be used on a hike.

Dehydrated foods, although they are cheaper than freeze-dried products, take longer to prepare and are less tasty. They are, however, improved by adding herbs and spices. If you can afford the extra weight of a fresh onion and a clove of garlic, they will make all the difference to a pasta dish. Packet soups provide the basis for a good meal, as do many instant sauces. Soya products have long been something most backpackers prefer to avoid at all costs, but this book attempts to provide recipes that even the staunchest non-believer will enjoy.

Remember, the important thing is to enjoy your food! Eat the right kind of food in the right quantities, prepared so that it is tasty, and your backpacking trip will be all the more enjoyable.

Note: Recipes marked ** are to be prepared at home, and those marked * are to be prepared partly at home.

USEFUL CONVERSIONS

Oven temperatures

70 °C – 150 °F
80 °C – 175 °F
100 °C – 200 °F
110 °C – 225 °F
120 °C – 250 °F
140 °C – 275 °F
150 °C – 300 °F
160 °C – 325 °F
180 °C – 350 °F
190 °C – 375 °F
200 °C – 400 °F
220 °C – 425 °F
230 °C – 450 °F
240 °C – 475 °F
260 °C – 500 °F

Very cool – 70 °C – 140 °C
Cool – 150 °C – 160 °C
Moderate – 180 °C – 190 °C
Moderately hot – 200 °C – 220 °C
Hot – 230 °C
Very hot – 240 °C – 260 °C

Weights

To make recipes as easy as possible for the hiker, measurements used in this book are, where possible, in the form of

15

cups, tablespoons and teaspoons. The table below shows the equivalent weight in grams and millilitres of 1 cup for various foodstuffs.

Beans, dried 250 g
Butter and margarine 250 g
Cheese, grated 125 g
Cocoa 111 g
Coconut, desiccated 75 g
Coffee, ground 100 g
Cornflour 166 g
Mealiemeal, unsifted 166 g
Milk 250 ml
Oats 91 g
Plain flour 125 g
Raisins 188 g
Rice (uncooked) 250 g
Sugar (brown) 200 g
Sugar (white) 250 g
Water 250 ml

The following conversion table shows the equivalent in millilitres of cups, tablespoons and teaspoons.

1 teaspoon   –   5 ml
1 tablespoon –   15 ml
1 cup   –   250 ml
½ cup   –   125 ml

Substitute

1 cup milk – 4 tablespoons milk powder and 1 cup water

CUTLERY AND COOKING EQUIPMENT

The following list may serve as a useful reminder of what you will need on a hike:

Spoon, fork and knife
Teaspoon
Billycan (lid serves as plate)
Miniature tin opener
Gas stove
Waterbottle
Plastic mug
Matches (store in empty film cannister together with torn-off flint)
Dishcloth (also to lift hot pots off the stove/fire)
Scourer
Small plastic bottle with dishwashing liquid
Large plastic bag (for haybox cooking) or the inside of a wine box with tap removed and slit open on one side

TIPS FOR PACKING FOOD

- Always carry margarine or oil in a plastic screwtop bottle and put the bottle inside a plastic bag in case of leakage.
- Pack soya mince for emergencies as it is extremely lightweight.
- Add milk powder and sugar to cereals and package into daily quantities before starting out.
- Do not add sugar and milk powder to your coffee in one container. You might want to share with someone who doesn't take sugar or milk, and you'll have to carry extra milk powder and sugar for other dishes anyway.
- Pack all the ingredients for each dish together and label all packages. Pack each day's meals and snacks into a big supermarket bag and label the bags per day. Put day one's package on top so you don't have to rummage through your whole pack for a snack. This also ensures that food is kept dry in the event of rain or an unexpected swim!
- Discard superfluous wrappings. Should the wrapping have an essential recipe on it, cut it out and stick it onto the inner package with cellotape
- Fresh meat will last longer if you freeze it and then wrap it in several layers of newspaper. Place in a plastic bag and knot the bag closed. Keep parcel at the bottom of the backpack.
- Carry chocolate in your cooking pot, wrapped in a towel to prevent it from melting too much.
- Take margarine instead of butter, as milk-based products quickly become rancid. The margarine will keep cool if you store it in the cooking pot.
- Save sachets of vinegar, chutney, etc. obtained from fast-food shops to use when cooking on the hike.

NUTRITION

It is not necessary to know the nutritional value of every item in your pack to be well nourished on a hike. The following widely used guide will ensure that you are getting the correct amount to sustain you. Pack food for a day should include:

- Two servings of protein-rich foods (1 serving is 60 g cooked meat, 1 cup cooked soya beans or lentils, 4 tablespoons peanut butter, or 1 cup nuts or seeds).
- Four servings of fruits and vegetables (1 serving is 1 piece of fruit or ½ cup dehydrated vegetables (when cooked).
- Two servings of milk or milk products (1 serving is 4 tablespoons dried milk powder or 45 g cheese).
- Four servings of bread or cereals (1 serving is 1 slice of bread, ½ cup cereal or ½ cup cooked pasta).

The sample menu on the next page is an example of a nutritionally balanced and tasty diet for a group of three for three days using recipes found in this book.

BREAKFAST		LUNCH		DINNER	
Day 1					
Crunchy Granola	300 g	6 slices trail bread	375 g	Tagliatelle with salami and cheese	800 g
3 small oranges	400 g	135 g cheese	135 g	Chocolate fondue	510 g
		1 small tin tuna	95 g		
Day 2					
3 Oatso-Easy strawberry	105 g	6 sheets crispbread	190 g	3 instant soup packets	50 g
3 small apples	300 g	Biltong pâté	300 g	Bacon and noodles	520 g
		Fruit balls	150 g	Sliced apples with honey	300 g
		Tangy sunflower seeds	60 g		
Day 3					
Muesli	300 g	9 Provitas	90 g	Cream of sweetcorn soup	300 g
Stewed fruit	200 g	3 cheese portions	90 g	Biltong potjie	500 g
		Dried figs	125 g	Toasted marshmallows	50 g
		Spicy nuts	125 g	Brown Russian drink	150 g
		1 tin mussels	120 g		

Miscellaneous
Coffee/tea/milk powder/sugar/salt/pepper/herbs/spreads/snacks/powderd cool drinks/margarine   550 g

HOW TO COOK DEHYDRATED VEGETABLES

Dried vegetables are usually more tender if they have been soaked long enough to reabsorb most of their lost water. If they are placed directly into a boiling soup or stew and are cooked without being given time to plump, they will be tougher.

Use only as much water as necessary to cover the vegetables. Boiling water shortens the rehydration time, but cold water may be used. Soak the vegetables for about 30 minutes to 1 hour.

After rehydration, vegetables are ready to be cooked. Simmered vegetables are more tender than those cooked over high heat. In a fully rehydrated vegetable, the cooking time is about the same or slightly longer than it would be for the same fresh vegetable.

Add salt or seasonings after rather than before or at the beginning of cooking.

Vegetables can also be prepared according to the haybox cooking method, saving time as you combine the soaking and cooking time (see page 22), and you therefore do not have to soak the vegetables before cooking.

HAYBOX COOKING

One of the joys of backpacking is sitting around an open wood fire in the evening discussing the events of the day. The pleasure of this experience, however, lessens somewhat if you are the cook who has to prepare a tasty supper by torchlight without burning the food and then has to clean a smoke-blackened pot afterwards! In all probability there will be some burnt food to scrape out as well, especially if the meal contained some form of soya protein. In addition, on a well-frequented trail, you may be faced with the prospect of cooking all your food in one pot, because there may not be enough pots to go around.

All these problems can be circumvented by using the haybox cooking method. The principle of this method is that the pot is insulated against heat loss so that the food is cooked slowly in its own heat. The apparatus needed for this cooking method is found in every backpack: a billycan, a sleeping bag, a dishcloth or towel, a large plastic bag and a thermal blanket. (To combine the plastic bag and thermal blanket, the inside of a winebox can be used – remove top and slit bag open on one side.)

Once you have tried this method you will find it the quickest and easiest way to prepare meals. First try it at home to gain confidence.

Method

1. Bring food to the boil. Do not lift the lid or peep at the food before wrapping it up (to keep the heat and steam in the pot). It is essential that the wrapping must be done as quickly as possible so that the minimum of heat is lost.
2. Taking the pot from the heat, quickly wrap it in the dish-

cloth or towel and put it into a plastic bag (to prevent moisture reaching your sleeping bag). The thermal blanket is wrapped around next, preferably with the reflecting surface closest to the pot. Lastly, the sleeping bag is folded around several times.
3. Leave the food to cook for about an hour or more. Food may be left longer but will become cold if left too long since the wraps do not insulate as thoroughly as would a proper haybox.

This method of preparing food cannot be recommended strongly enough. There are several reasons for this:

- You can prepare your food within a few minutes and then go off to explore, swim or wash and come back to a lovely hot meal. Prepare the food as soon as you arrive at the hut and then relax.
- Soups, stews, casseroles, dried vegetables and fruit stews are all admirable subjects for haybox cooking. It is unnecessary to soak dehydrated foodstuff before cooking when using the haybox method. It is also ideal for preparing a complete meal in one pot. With a little ingenuity you can adapt any of your favourite casserole dishes to haybox cooking.
- The flavour of food is much improved by the extended slow cooking.
- The food doesn't burn and you don't have to worry about scouring the pot afterwards.
- It saves gas when fuel is at a premium on long hikes.
- It enables you to be independent of equipment on the well-frequented trails where you often have to wait your turn with pots and the fire.

HASSLE-FREE INSTANT MEALS

The following instant foods are suggestions for those meals where you are unable or do not want to cook. Obviously similar products with different brand names may be used. The purpose of this section is not to be complete, but rather to set your mind alive and to make you aware of the possibilities of the items on the supermarket shelves.

Breakfast

- Pro-Nutro (For each serving, mix 1 cup Pro-Nutro with 2 teaspoons sugar and 1 tablespoon milk powder. Add hot or cold water.)
- Eggs. Take fresh eggs in their own containers, or buy plastic containers at your camping store. Pack carefully on top of your backpack in a plastic bag and inside a towel or sleeping bag. Eat on the first day.
- Weetbix. Use 2 teaspoons sugar and 1 tablespoon milk powder per serving. Add hot or cold water.
- Granola bar. Simply enjoy with coffee.
- Oatso-Easy hot oats. The secret is to add enough water to ensure that the mixture isn't gooey. The strawberry and cream flavour is especially delicious and is even nicer with a chopped fresh banana on top.
- Golden Harvest products: Honey Crunch, Muesli, Vita Trim, Nutti Crunch, Fruit 'n Fibre, Nutti Nola, Yogi Crunch, Bran Crunch.

Lunch

- Renown individual mini-polonies (eat on first day).
- John West French pork liver pâté.
- Glenryck pilchards in hot chilli sauce.
- Goldcrest smoked mussels in vegetable oil.
- Towerkop pepperoni cheese smear.
- Bakers snackbread.
- Portuguese sardines in vegetable oil.
- John West sardines in vegetable oil.
- Aida Delicatess bread for cheese.
- Wechshof Camembert cheese.
- Fresh fruit: apples and oranges keep best.
- Provita.
- Salami.
- Dried wors and biltong.
- Cheddar cheese to top bread and crackers, and to grate into one-pot dinners and soups.

Dinner

- Royco pasta and sauce.
- Knorr easy packet sauces.
- Golden Dragon noodle sticks/Chinese Mien.
- Knorr pasta sauce mix.
- Tastic savoury classics rice.
- Woolworths' Potato and sausage sauté, Scalloped potato with onion and bacon, Bubble and squeak.
- Bacon bits (bacon flavoured soya): add to soups and dinners.
- Lentils: nutritious and lightweight. Cook according to the haybox method with rice and curry powder for a hassle-free, nutritious meal.
- Smash: use for the main meal or as a thickener and in soups. Add grated nutmeg for a nice change.

- Take along chutney, coconut and dehydrated bananas to serve with curry.
- Royco Italiano sauces.
- Premix salt, pepper, dried garlic and other herbs with rice, noodles, soups and other dishes before setting out.
- Royco international Chinese sweet and sour instant sauce, served with tuna.
- Pasta Romagna cheese-filled tortellini.
- Pasta Romagna meat-filled ravioli.
- Radiated food from the Atomic Energy Corporation. Phone (012) 316 5313 (Dr Harold Brodrick) for more details.

Desserts

- Roast marshmallows in the fire or over a candle flame.
- Mix instant pudding or custard powder with full-cream milk powder and water (1½ cups of cold water to 3 tablespoons of milk powder). Add coconut, chocolate, chopped nuts or dried fruit.
- Pack biscuits (such as Nuttikrust toffee flavoured biscuits) in a bowl, and pour over liqueur (such as Eine Kleine Nachtmusik or Harry's Cape Velvet (see page 120)). Serve with custard.
- Simply open a packet of Albany Tinkers and enjoy.
- Add custard to Golden Harvest Nutti Nola.
- Sprinkle Golden Harvest Nutti Nola or Yogi Crunch over a small tin of fruit salad.
- Finger biscuits weigh almost nothing and can be served in a variety of ways – let your imagination run riot.
- Open a can of Carnation Treat (caramel or chocolate flavour) and dig in with your spoons, or smear onto biscuits.
- Mix Post Toasties, flaked almonds and condensed milk for a lovely (but very sweet!) treat.
- Soak prunes in brandy for an hour or two and serve with

custard or a small tin of cream or evaporated milk.
- Chocolite instant hot chocolate drink.

Snacks

The list of snacks one could take on a hike is obviously inexhaustible and the following are just a few suggestions:

- Dried fruit: SAD Smyrna figs, Mango Man pineapple, Safari Bulida apricots, mebos, minced fruit cubes, minced fruit croquettes.
- Mix nuts, raisins and Smarties.
- Woolworths' Streaky Bacon Snacks.
- SAD's Cedric the Crow Fruit Chips.
- Dairy Belle's individually packed Country Style Cheddar (20 portions of 30 g each).
- PVM Apple bars.
- Woolworths' Tropical Chewy Bar with banana, mango and pineapple.
- Biltong and dried wors.

CEREALS AND PORRIDGE

Basic Granola**

>	2 cups wholewheat flour
>	6 cups rolled oats
>	1 cup desiccated coconut
>	1 cup wheat germ
>	1/2 cup water
>	1 cup oil
>	1/2 cup syrup or honey
>	2 teaspoons vanilla
>	1 tablespoon salt

Combine all dry ingredients in one bowl and liquid ingredients in another. Add liquid to dry ingredients and mix thoroughly. Spread on two greased baking sheets. Bake for 1 hour at 120 °C or until golden brown and dry. Store in a covered container. A variety of dried fruits, nuts and seeds can be added.

Serves 24

Crunchy Breakfast Mix**

>	350 g muesli base (see page 31)
>	50 g wheat germ
>	50 g bran
>	50 g sunflower seeds
>	50 g sesame seeds
>	50 g desiccated coconut
>	6 tablespoons sunflower oil
>	raisins, sultanas and broken banana chips to taste

Heat the oven to 180 °C. Mix together the muesli base, wheat germ, bran, sunflower and sesame seeds, coconut and oil. Spread the mixture in a large, flat oven tin and bake for 45 minutes, turning the mixture several times.

Tip the cereal into a flat dish and cool completely. Store in an airtight container.

Before serving, mix in raisins, sultanas and broken banana chips. The cereal can be eaten dry or with milk.

*Crunchy Granola***

> 4 cups rolled oats (not instant)
> 1 cup wheat germ
> 1/2 cup bran flakes
> 1 cup desiccated coconut
> 1/4 cup sesame seeds
> 1/2 cup sunflower seeds
> 1/2 teaspoon cinnamon
> 1/8 teaspoon salt
> 1 tablespoon oil
> 1/2 cup honey
> 1/2 cup apple juice or water
> 1/2 cup brown sugar
> 2 tablespoons vanilla essence
> 2 cups chopped dried fruit
> 1 cup chopped nuts

Preheat oven to 150 °C. Mix oats, wheat germ, bran flakes, coconut, sesame seeds, sunflower seeds, cinnamon and salt. In a pan, heat oil, honey, apple juice or water and brown sugar until warm, stirring until brown sugar is dissolved. Remove from heat and stir in vanilla. Pour oil mixture over oat mixture, stirring to mix well. Pour into a shallow baking pan and bake for 25 to 30 minutes or until golden brown, stirring every 10 minutes. During last 5 minutes of baking stir in dried fruit and nuts. Cool and store in airtight container at room temperature. Use within 4 weeks.

Makes about 9 cups

*Fruit and Nut Muesli***

> 75 g dried apricots
> 75 g dates
> 75 g almonds
> 75 g walnuts
> 40 g sunflower seeds
> 325 g rolled oats

Roughly chop the apricots and dates. Finely chop the almonds and walnuts. Toast the sunflower seeds and mix all ingredients with the oats. Stir together thoroughly and store in an airtight container.

Serves 8

*Muesli Base***

> 450 g jumbo rolled oats
> 350 g rolled wheat
> 350 g rolled barley
> 350 g rolled rye

Thoroughly mix the cereals together. Store in an airtight container. Nuts and dried fruit can be added to taste.

*Muesli I***

>   500 g rolled oats
>   75 g bran
>   125 g raisins
>   100 g almonds
>   125 g sunflower seeds
>   100 g soft brown sugar
>   100 g milk powder

Mix ingredients and store in an airtight container. Serve with hot or cold water.

Serves 8

*Muesli II***

>   2 cups rolled oats
>   1 cup bran flakes
>   2 tablespoons wheat germ
>   1/4 cup bran
>   1/2 cup seedless raisins
>   1/2 cup dried apples, cut into small pieces
>   1/2 cup dried apricots or peaches, cut into small pieces
>   1/2 cup mixed nuts or sunflower seeds, chopped finely
>   1/2 cup skimmed milk powder

Mix all the ingredients well and store in an airtight container.

Makes 6 cups

Oatmeal Porridge

For a simple bowl of porridge, place about 2 tablespoons of oats and a pinch of salt in a saucepan with ⅔ cup water or skimmed milk and stir over moderate heat for 3–5 minutes until thick and creamy. Raisins and other fruit may be added for extra nutrition.

BREAD AND RUSKS

Bran Rusks**

>   2 eggs
>   2 cups brown sugar
>   500 g margarine, melted
>   1 kg self-raising flour
>   1 teaspoon salt
>   1 tablespoon baking powder
>   2 cups buttermilk
>   5 cups All Bran flakes

Beat eggs and sugar together. Add margarine. Mix all dry ingredients together, except bran flakes. Add dry ingredients to egg and sugar mixture alternately with the buttermilk. Add bran flakes and mix well. Smooth mixture into a greased pan and bake at 180 °C for 40 minutes. Cut into squares and place in a slow oven (100 °C) for up to 6 hours until crisp.

Makes 48

Chapatis

>   2 cups Nutty Wheat flour
>   1/4 cup water
>   oil or margarine

Blend the flour with just enough water to form a stiff dough. Knead the dough until smooth and elastic. Place in a pot and cover with a damp cloth. Allow to rest for 2–3 hours, if possible. Knead the dough once more and divide into 6 equal pieces, each about the size of an egg. Shape each piece into a flat, round patty and roll out thinly (use any cylindrical object such as an empty film cannister or clean gas container). Heat the oil or margarine and fry each chapati until brown spots appear on the side being fried. Flip and repeat. Remove from the heat and butter one side. Wrap the chapatis in a clean cloth to keep them soft and warm until they are served.

Makes 6

Garlic Bread

Mix salt and garlic powder (according to taste) with margarine and spread on slices of bread. Toast over hot coals or wrap in tinfoil and heat over coals until margarine has melted.

Indian Coconut Bread

1/4 cup desiccated coconut
1/2 teaspoon salt
1/4 cup cake flour
pinch cayenne pepper
1/2 teaspoon castor sugar
2 tablespoons water
oil or margarine

Place dry ingredients in a mixing bowl. Mix in the water and blend to form a fairly stiff dough. Divide the dough into 6 equal portions and shape each into a flat patty about 75 mm in diameter. Heat the oil or margarine and fry the coconut cakes carefully until golden brown on both sides.

Makes 6 cakes

Nutty Yoghurt Bread**

>3 eggs
>1/2 cup soft brown sugar
>7 cups Nutty Wheat flour
>1 cup molasses bran
>1 cup unsalted peanuts
>1/2 cup sesame seeds
>1/2 cup sunflower seeds
>1 1/2 teaspoons baking powder
>2 teaspoons salt
>1 cup plain yoghurt
>1 cup milk
>extra sesame seeds

Beat together eggs and sugar until thick and pale. Add remaining ingredients to give a dropping consistency. Spoon mixture into a large, greased loaf pan. Sprinkle with sesame seeds. Bake at 180 °C for 1–1½ hours or until a skewer inserted into the centre comes out clean. Leave to cool on cooling rack.

Makes one loaf

Quick Bread Mix**

>1,5 kg white bread flour
>4 teaspoons salt
>1 1/2 teaspoons bicarbonate of soda
>4 teaspoons baking powder
>1 tablespoon cream of tartar
>1 1/4 cup coffee creamer
>500 g margarine

Sift the dry ingredients together into a large mixing bowl and mix well. Cut in the margarine with a knife, then rub it in to form a crumbly mixture. Place in a large airtight container and store in a cool, dry place.

To make bread, simple add enough water to achieve the correct consistency, place the dough in a greased loaf pan and bake at 180 °C for an hour or until the loaf makes a hollow sound when tapped.

The bread can be sliced and taken on the trail for the first two days, or the mix can be made into rolls.

Makes 2 loaves or 24 rolls

Alternatively, take the mix on trail and prepare stick bread:

Stick Bread

> 2 cups quick bread mix (see above)
> ¼ cup water

Mix the bread mix to a soft dough with the water. Mould small quantities of dough into spirals around skewers or clean sticks (not dry sticks or they will burn!) making sure the dough covers the end of the sticks. 'Bake' on a grid over low coals for 15–20 minutes, turning often. Slip the bread off the stick and serve with margarine in the hollow.

Makes 4–6

Trail Bread**

> 5 cups wholewheat flour
> 1 teaspoon bicarbonate of soda
> 1 tablespoon sunflower seeds
> 1 tablespoon sesame seeds
> 1 tablespoon linseed
> 1 tablespoon digestive bran
> 2 tablespoons brown sugar
> 2 teaspoons molasses
> 2 cups buttermilk

Combine all ingredients except molasses and buttermilk. Mix well. Add molasses and buttermilk. Mix well. Pour into greased loaf tin and bake at 180 °C for 1½ hours.

Makes 1 loaf

Yoghurt Bran Bread**

> 1¼ cup self-raising flour
> 1¼ cup Nutty Wheat flour
> ¼ cup digestive bran
> ¾ cup brown sugar
> ½ teaspoon nutmeg
> ½ teaspoon salt
> 1 teaspoon bicarbonate of soda
> ¼ cup seedless raisins
> ¼ cup walnuts, chopped
> 1 egg
> 1 teaspoon vanilla essence
> 4 tablespoons oil
> 185 ml plain yoghurt

Mix together dry ingredients. In a separate bowl, lightly whisk remaining ingredients. Stir in dry ingredients. Spoon mixture into a 10 × 20 cm loaf pan and bake at 180 °C for 1 hour or until cooked.

Serves 8

SPREADS AND PÂTÉS

Biltong Pâté I**

>   285 g tin creamed mushrooms
>   2 onions, chopped
>   30 g butter or margarine
>   300 g grated biltong
>   200 ml mayonnaise
>   50 ml cream cheese
>   2 ml black pepper
>   2 ml nutmeg
>   1 ml cloves

Sauté onion in the butter or margarine. Add all the other ingredients and blend in a food processor.

Biltong Pâté II**

>   1 tablespoon oil
>   1 onion, chopped
>   200 g button mushrooms, wiped and chopped
>   2 cups grated biltong
>   1/2 cup cream/cottage cheese
>   3/4 cup mayonnaise
>   2 tablespoons chopped parsley

Sauté onion and mushrooms. Add remaining ingredients and allow to cool slightly. Place mixture in a blender until smooth.

Cheese Spread

>5 teaspoons Farmer's Pride Cheddar cheese powder
>1/4 teaspoon mustard powder

Mix the cheese and mustard powder with a little bit of warm water to form a smooth paste. Spread on savoury biscuits for a delicious snack.

Energy Smear**

>410 g peanut butter
>1/4–1/2 cup cooking oil (depending on oiliness of peanut butter)
>1/2 cup honey
>500 g–1 kg powdered milk (depending on oiliness of peanut butter)

Mix all the ingredients to a soft fudge. Store in airtight containers. Chopped nuts, dates and raisins can also be added, if required.

Makes about 1–1,5 kg

Fig Sandwich Spread

Soak dry figs in water until soft. Chop and sweeten with a little honey. Combine with chopped nuts. Can also be used as a filling for dessert (see cornflake flan, page 111).

Green Bean and Walnut Pâté**

> 1/4 cup butter
> 1 onion, chopped
> 500 g green beans, trimmed, boiled and drained
> 2 eggs, hard boiled and shelled
> 1/4 cup chopped walnuts
> salt and pepper

Heat butter and sauté onion until soft. Place in blender, add remaining ingredients except seasoning and blend until smooth. Season to taste. Spoon mixture into a plastic screwtop bottle and serve with savoury cheese wafers.

Peanut Butter**

> 1 cup peanuts
> 2 tablespoons oil
> dash of salt

Blend peanuts with oil until smooth and add salt. Add 60 ml sunflower or sesame seeds for a different flavour and 60 ml dried fruit for a chewier texture.

Peanut Butter Filling**

Add chopped dates, raisins or dried figs to peanut butter and serve on melba toast, rice cakes or other bread substitute.

Peanut Butter and Fruit Spread**

1 cup peanut butter
2 tablespoons margarine
1/3 cup finely chopped dried fruit
1 tablespoon lemon juice
2 tablespoons honey

Combine all ingredients and mix until smooth. Serve on crackers or bread.

NUTS AND SEEDS

*Candied Orange Pecans***

>   1 1/2 cup light brown sugar
>   1 cup orange juice
>   225 g pecan halves
>   grated rind of 1 large orange
>   3 tablespoons butter or margarine

Oil a marble sheet or baking sheet. Put the sugar and juice in a saucepan and stir over a low heat until the sugar is dissolved. Bring to the boil and keep boiling until the syrup has reached the soft ball stage. When it begins to thicken and reduce, test a few drops in a cup of cold water. When they form soft balls remove from heat and immediately add the grated rind and butter or margarine. Beat with a wooden spoon until the mixture begins to stiffen. Quickly add the pecans and continue stirring until they look sugary. Turn out on the oiled surface and separate the nuts, using two forks. Dry on a rack.

*Curried Nuts***

>   750 g nuts
>   2 tablespoons vegetable oil
>   2 heaped tablespoons fresh curry powder
>   1 teaspoon soy sauce
>   1 teaspoon Worcestershire sauce
>   1 teaspoon garlic powder
>   salt

Place the nuts in a shallow pan. Mix the oil, curry powder, soy sauce, Worcestershire sauce and garlic together and pour over the nuts. Stir well with a wooden spoon. Bake in a moderate oven for 15–20 minutes, stirring frequently, or sauté in a frying pan. The nuts should take on colour but not burn. Spread on paper towels to drain and sprinkle on the salt.

*Mexican Nuts***

>1/4 cup butter or margarine, melted
>1 1/4 teaspoons chilli powder
>1/2 teaspoon coriander
>1/2 teaspoon paprika
>1/4 teaspoon salt
>dash cumin
>4 cups mixed nuts

Preheat oven to 135 °C. Mix melted butter or margarine, chilli powder, coriander, paprika, salt and cumin. Add nuts and stir well. Spread mixture in a shallow baking pan and bake for 20–25 minutes, stirring occasionally. Drain on paper towels.

Makes 4 cups

*Roasted Soya Beans***

>500 g soya beans
>1 tablespoon margarine
>1/2 teaspoon salt

Soak soya beans overnight. Drain and dry. Heat beans until golden in a heavy frying pan, stirring constantly. Add margarine and salt. Stir until soya beans are well coated. Drain on absorbent paper and store in a closed container.

Seed Snacks**

1 cup squash or pumpkin seeds
1 tablespoon melted margarine
1 teaspoon Worcestershire sauce
salt to taste

Save up squash and pumpkin seeds for this treat. Cover with water and boil for 5–10 minutes. Drain, making sure seeds are free of fibres. Combine margarine and Worcestershire sauce, dribble over seeds and mix. Place on a baking sheet. Sprinkle with salt. Bake at 180 °C for 30 minutes or until dry.

Spicy Nuts I**

750 g nuts
2 tablespoons vegetable oil
1 heaped tablespoon masala
salt

Place the nuts in a shallow pan. Mix the oil and masala together and pour over the nuts. Stir well with a wooden spoon. Bake in a moderate oven for 15–20 minutes, stirring frequently, or sauté in a frying pan. The nuts should take on colour but not burn. Spread on paper towels to drain and sprinkle on the salt. The flavour improves by the following day.

Spicy Nuts II**

> 3 tablespoons butter or margarine, melted
> 1/2 teaspoon seasoned salt
> 1/4 teaspoon garlic salt
> 1/4 teaspoon paprika
> 1/8 teaspoon onion powder
> dash Tabasco sauce
> 3 cups mixed nuts

Preheat oven to 135 °C. In a medium bowl, mix melted butter or margarine, seasoned salt, garlic salt, paprika, onion powder and Tabasco sauce. Add nuts and mix well. Spread mixture in a shallow baking pan. Bake in preheated oven for 20–25 minutes, stirring occasionally. Drain on paper towels.

Makes 3 cups

Sugar and Spice Nuts**

> 1 egg white
> 1 tablespoon butter or margarine, melted
> 3 cups mixed nuts (almonds, cashews, peanuts, pecans, sunflower seeds and walnuts)
> 3/4 cup sugar
> 2 tablespoons cornflour
> 1 1/2 teaspoons cinnamon
> 1/2 teaspoon ground allspice
> 1/2 teaspoon nutmeg
> 1/4 teaspoon salt

Preheat oven to 135 °C. In a small bowl, lightly beat egg white. Stir in melted butter or margarine. Add nuts and stir to coat with egg white mixture. In a separate bowl, mix sugar, cornflour, cinnamon, allspice, nutmeg and salt. Add nuts to spice mixture. Stir until all nuts are coated. Spread mixture in a shallow baking pan. Bake in preheated oven for 45 minutes. Break apart while still warm.

Makes 3½ cups

*Tangy Sunflower Seeds***

    2 tablespoons vegetable oil
    1 tablespoon soy sauce
    ¼ teaspoon paprika
    ½ teaspoon celery salt
    dash cayenne pepper
    2 cups raw sunflower kernels

Preheat oven to 150 °C. Mix oil, soy sauce, paprika, celery salt and cayenne pepper. Add sunflower kernels and stir until they are evenly coated. Spread mixture in a shallow baking pan and bake for 20 minutes, stirring frequently. Drain on paper towels.

Makes 2 cups

FRUIT NIBBLES

*Apple Snack***

Peel, core and halve as many apples as you need. Shred coarsely and spread on an oiled baking sheet. Bake at 110 °C until dry. Remove from baking sheet with a spatula and break into pieces. Store in a covered container. Add to trail mixes, hot and cold cereals and desserts or eat as they are.

*Apricotlets***

> 1³⁄4 cups boiling water
> 1¹⁄3 cups dried apricots
> 2 cups white sugar
> 2 tablespoons golden syrup
> 1⁄8 teaspoon salt
> 2 tablespoons unflavoured gelatin
> 1⁄2 cup apple juice
> 1 teaspoon lemon juice
> 3⁄4 cup chopped nuts
> castor sugar

Lightly coat a square baking pan with butter or margarine. Set aside. Pour boiling water over apricots and stand until apricots are plump (about 30 minutes). Blend water and apricots to a pulp in blender. Put through a sieve and discard fiber and skin. Simmer pulp, sugar, syrup and salt in a saucepan over low heat, stirring occasionally to prevent scorching.

Dissolve gelatin in apple juice. Stir into pulp mixture and again cook until thickened (about 10 minutes). Stir in lemon juice and chopped nuts. Pour mixture into prepared pan. Stand at room temperature for 24 hours and then cut into bars. If knife sticks, dip it in hot water. Place bars on a tray in a warm place until dry to touch. Roll in castor sugar.

Makes 36 pieces

*Apricot Jujubes***

>1 cup sun-dried apricots
>approximately 1/2 cup icing sugar
>1 tablespoon ground coriander
>2–3 tablespoons rum or brandy
>shelled pistachio nuts

Put the apricots through a mincer or food processor until they are finely chopped. Place in a mixing bowl, add the icing sugar a little at a time, and knead with your hands until the mixture is fairly stiff. Add the coriander and rum or brandy. The mixture should be moist but not sloppy.

Shape into marble-sized balls, roll in the remaining icing sugar and place a peeled pistachio nut in the centre of each ball. Leave overnight to dry and then store in an airtight container.

*Apricot Sweets***

>225 g dried apricots
>150 ml unsweetened orange juice
>75 g raisins
>100 g sunflower seeds
>rice paper

Soak the apricots in the orange juice for 2 hours. Drain. Finely mince the apricots with the raisins and sunflower seeds. Work the mixture well with your fingers. Roll out the mixture between sheets of rice paper to a thickness of 6 mm. Leave for 2 hours to set firm and cut into 2,5 cm squares or small bars.

Blind Dates

1 packet dried, stoned dates
salted peanuts (not dry-roasted)
white sugar

Cut a slit in each date and fill with salted peanuts. Roll in sugar.

Filled Fruit Rolls

Unroll a fruit roll (it must be soft and pliable, not brittle) and spread with one of the following fillings:

Melted chocolate
Cheddar cheese spread
Fruit jam
Marmalade
Peanut butter

Roll up the fruit roll again and cut into bite-size pieces.

*Fruit Balls***

1/4 cup dried apricots
1/2 cup dried figs
1 cup dried dates
1/2 cup dried prunes
1/4 cup raisins
1/3 cup desiccated coconut
1/3 cup sunflower seeds
1 cup finely chopped nuts
3 tablespoons lemon juice
2 tablespoons syrup

In blender or food mixer, finely chop apricots, figs, dates, prunes and raisins. In a medium bowl, mix finely chopped fruit with coconut, sunflower seeds and nuts. Stir in lemon juice. Add syrup gradually and mix well. Shape into balls and dry in oven for 4–6 hours until firm to touch.

Makes 36 balls

*Fruit Rolls***

1 cup dried figs
1 cup pitted dates
1 cup seedless raisins
1 1/2 cups chopped nuts
2 tablespoons lemon juice

Grind fruit in a food processor. Mix with nuts and lemon juice and shape into small rolls.

Makes 24 rolls

Golden Crunch Balls**

1/2 cup dried apricots
1/2 cup dried apples
1/2 cup dried peaches
1/2 cup desiccated coconut
1/4 cup blanched almonds
1 teaspoon grated lemon rind
1/2 teaspoon cinnamon
3 tablespoons honey
3 tablespoons orange juice
1 tablespoon lemon juice
castor sugar, if desired

Grind apricots, apples and peaches in blender until pieces are the size of rock salt or finer. Place in a medium bowl and stir in coconut, almonds, lemon rind and cinnamon. In a small saucepan, slightly warm honey, orange juice and lemon juice. Stir to mix well. Slowly pour honey mixture over fruit mixture, stirring until mixture sticks together evenly. Form into small balls and place on baking sheets. Dry in oven at 50 °C until no longer sticky to touch (up to 6 hours). If desired, roll balls in castor sugar.

Makes 48 balls

Mixed Fruit Snack**

1/2 cup dried apples
1/2 cup dried apricots
1/4 cup dried peaches
1/2 cup dried pears
1/2 cup dried pineapple
1/4 cup desiccated coconut
1/2 cup raisins
1/2 cup cashews or almonds

Cut apples, apricots, peaches, pears and pineapple into small pieces and combine all ingredients in a bowl. Package in airtight plastic bags and store in a cool, dry place. Use within 3–4 weeks.

Makes about 3½ cups

*Orange Peel in Syrup***

peel of 6 large, thin-skinned oranges
2 cups sugar
2 cups water
1 tablespoon lemon juice

Scrape the surface of the oranges with a fork, then peel from top to bottom with a sharp knife to make 6 segment strips. Scrape off the excess pith from the peel, then boil the peel until soft (approximately 30 minutes). Drain well and soak in cold water for 24 hours, changing the water several times.

Roll up each strip and with a large needle, thread onto a heavy cotton thread, making a 'necklace' to prevent the rolls from unravelling.

Bring the sugar and water to the boil, add the lemon juice and continue to boil for a further 5 minutes. Drop the 'necklace' into the boiling syrup, turn down the heat and simmer slowly, stirring occasionally with a wooden spoon, until the syrup thickens enough to thickly coat the back of the spoon.

Lift the necklace out of the syrup, remove the thread and drop the rolls into a jar. Allow the syrup to cool slightly, then pour over the rolls, making sure they are all covered. Seal with an airtight lid.

Serve the rolls either with the syrup or rolled in sugar as crystallised fruit.

Makes a lovely snack on trail, but can also be served as dessert.

Peanut Butter and Banana Leather**

>   1 cup peanut butter
>   1 cup mashed, ripe bananas
>   2 tablespoons honey

Blend all ingredients together. Spread mixture thinly on a sheet of waxed paper 1 metre long. Place on baking rack. Leave in a dry place with air circulating for 2–3 days until the mixture is dry and resembles leather. Roll up strips of the mixture or flake and put in a plastic bag.

Sesame Fruit Balls**

>   250 g pitted dates
>   1/3 cup seedless raisins
>   250 g dried apricots
>   1/4 cup sesame seeds

Grind fruit in a food processor, then shape into small balls. Roll in sesame seeds or any desired covering.

Makes 24 balls

Stuffed Prunes

>   1 packet pitted prunes
>   1 cup sunflower seeds

Fill prune cavities with sunflower seeds.

Surprise Prunes**

500 g large pitted prunes
crystallised ginger or citron
grated peel of 2 oranges
½ cup white sugar

Cut the ginger or citron into thick slivers and fill each prune. Mix the grated peel with the sugar and roll the prunes one at a time in the mixture until they are covered. Leave on a plate to dry for several hours, then pack in an airtight container.

ENERGY BARS AND SWEET NIBBLES

*Almond Squares***

>*1/3 cup honey*
>*1/3 cup oil*
>*1/2 cup wholewheat flour*
>*1/2 cup soy flour*
>*1/2 cup wheat germ*
>*1 tablespoon nutritional yeast*
>*2 eggs, beaten*
>*1/2 cup almonds, ground*
>*1 cup desiccated coconut*
>*1/2 cup dried fruit, chopped*

Blend honey and oil. Stir in wholewheat and soy flour, wheat germ and yeast. Pat mixture into bottom of oiled pan. Bake at 180 °C for 10 minutes. Remove from oven and allow to cool. Beat eggs, almonds, coconut and fruit together. Pour mixture over baked crust, return to oven and bake at same heat for another 25 minutes. Cut into squares when cool.

Makes 12 squares

*Apricot Coconut Bars***

>*100 g soft margarine*
>*100 g castor sugar*
>*100 g self-raising flour*
>*2 eggs*
>*75 g desiccated coconut*
>*100 g dried apricots*

Put margarine, sugar, flour, eggs and half the coconut into a bowl. Beat well until smooth. Spoon coconut mixture into a greased (18 × 28 × 4 cm) baking tin and level the top. Finely chop apricots and mix with remaining coconut. Sprinkle over mixture in tin.

Bake at 180 °C for 30 minutes until well risen. Leave to cool.

Makes 15 bars

*Brazil Nut Bars***

100 g shelled brazil nuts
100 g glazed figs
100 g stoned dates
rice paper

Finely mince together the brazil nuts, figs and dates. Work the mixture well with your fingers to ensure the ingredients are evenly mixed. Roll out the mixture between sheets of rice paper to a thickness of 6 mm. Cut into 2,5 cm squares or small bars.

*Chewy Hazelnut Bars***

100 g shelled hazelnuts, finely chopped
225 g muesli base (see page 31)
75 g sultanas
100 g light brown sugar
2 tablespoons honey
125 ml sunflower oil

Preheat the oven to 200 °C. Mix together the hazelnuts, muesli base and sultanas. Put the sugar, honey and oil into a saucepan and set on a low heat. Stir until the honey and sugar have melted and the oil is well blended in. Add the hazelnut mixture and mix well.

Press the mixture into a well-oiled 20 × 28 cm baking tin. Bake for 10 minutes. Cut the mixture into bars and leave in the tin until the bars are just warm so they set into shape. Remove to a wire rack or a flat plate and leave to cool.

*Crispy Date Bars***

250 g butter or margarine
500 g dates, chopped
200 g sugar
240 g Rice Krispies
50 ml desiccated coconut

In a large saucepan, melt butter and sugar and add dates. Stir constantly until soft and smooth. Remove from heat. Add Rice Krispies and stir until combined. Press into a greased 27 × 37 cm baking pan. Cover with sheet of greaseproof paper. Roll with rolling pin to compress. Remove paper, sprinkle with coconut and cut into bars.

Makes 50 pieces

*Date Pinwheels***

Date filling (see page 112)
1/2 cup butter or margarine
1/2 cup brown sugar
1/2 cup white sugar
1 egg
1 teaspoon vanilla essence
2 cups plain flour
1/4 teaspoon baking soda
1/4 teaspoon salt

Prepare date filling, increasing nuts to 1 cup. In a medium bowl, cream butter or margarine with brown and white sugar. Add egg and vanilla. Beat well. In a separate bowl, mix flour, baking soda and salt. Add to creamed mixture and mix well. Cut dough in half. Generously flour a large sheet of wax paper. Roll out each half of dough on floured wax paper. Spread with filling. Starting with longer edge, roll up tightly to make a long roll. Wrap roll in wax paper. Refrigerate for at least 4 hours, preferably overnight.

Preheat oven to 190 °C. Grease baking sheets and set aside. Cut chilled roll into slices. Place slices on prepared baking sheets and bake in oven for 8–10 minutes until edges are golden.

Makes about 80 cookies

*Date Squares***

1 cup granadilla Liquifruit
180 g dates, chopped
1 teaspoon bicarbonate of soda
pinch salt
125 g margarine
230 g castor sugar
1 egg
250 g flour
1/2 teaspoon vanilla essence

Boil Liquifruit and pour over chopped dates. Add bicarbonate of soda and salt. Leave to cool. In a separate bowl, cream castor sugar and margarine together. Add egg and beat well. Add the date mixture and flour alternately to egg mixture. Add vanilla essence. Stir well after each addition.

Pour mixture into Swiss roll tin (34 × 21 cm) and bake at 160 °C for 1 hour. Cut into squares.

Energy Bars**

500 g stoned dates
250 g seedless raisins
250 g sultanas
200 g salted peanuts
1/4 cup sunflower kernels

Mix half of the fruit and peanuts and put in blender until smooth. Add rest of ingredients and work through with fingers. Press mixture on a lightly greased pan to 1 cm thick. Mark the bars with a knife. Cool until set and then break into bars. Wrap separately in waxpaper or cling wrap.

Makes 30 bars

Fig Fudge**

250 g dried figs
250 g ground almonds
75 g cocoa powder
1 teaspoon cinnamon
grated rind of 1 lemon
250 g white sugar
1/2 cup water

Mince the figs finely or put them through a food processor. Assemble the rest of the dry ingredients, except for the sugar, in a mixing bowl. Combine the sugar and water in a heavy saucepan. Bring to the boil, stirring only until the sugar is dissolved. Then boil without stirring for a minute or two, until it has thickened and is slightly reduced. Remove from heat and beat in the remaining ingredients. The mixture will be very stiff. Return to the heat and cook gently until it is slightly shiny and comes away from the sides and bottom of the pan in a mass. (This takes only a few minutes.) Pat into a shallow dish, allow to cool and cut into squares. Sprinkle with sugar.

*Fruit and Nut Bars***

> 60 g butter or margarine
> 200 g packet marshmallows (use the soft round brand)
> 75 g Rice Krispies
> 125 g dried apricots, finely chopped
> 50 g unsalted peanuts

Melt butter in a pan, add marshmallows and stir until melted. Add Rice Krispies, apricots and peanuts and mix well. Transfer mixture to a shallow, square dish and press down gently with a hot metal spoon. Cut into squares when cool.

Makes 15 squares

*Fruit Bars***

> 450 g stoned dates, prunes, apricots or figs
> 200 g sugar
> 150 ml syrup
> 50 ml orange juice
> 2 teaspoons grated orange rind
> 1 teaspoon salt
> 1 teaspoon bicarbonate of soda
> 300 g flour
> 240 g margarine
> 200 g brown sugar
> 120 ml water
> 100 g oats

Combine fruit, sugar, orange juice, rind and 1 ml salt and cook until thick. Cool. Sift together the flour, bicarb and salt. Rub in the margarine, add the brown sugar and water. Beat until smooth. Fold in the oats. Spread half the mixture over the bottom of a baking tray. Cover with fruit filling. Roll out remaining mixture and place over filling. Bake at 180 °C for 30–35 minutes. Cool and cut into bars.

Makes 36

*Fruit Crunchies***

240 g flour
500 ml oats
150 g raisins
160 g coconut
300 g brown sugar
½ teaspoon salt
250 g margarine
2 tablespoons golden syrup
1 egg, beaten
1 teaspoon vanilla essence
1 teaspoon bicarbonate of soda dissolved in a little milk

Combine flour, oats, raisins, coconut, brown sugar and salt. Melt margarine and syrup together. Add egg, vanilla and bicarbonate of soda. Combine wet and dry ingredients. Press mixture into a greased 300 mm baking tray. Bake at 180 °C for 20 minutes.

Makes 36

Knapsack Cookies

2 cups oats
pinch salt
pinch bicarbonate of soda
1 tablespoon melted margarine
warm water

Mix oats, salt and bicarbonate of soda with melted margarine and enough warm water to bind the mixture. Knead into a round shape and press to 1 cm thick on a flat surface sprinkled with oats. Cut in squares and bake on a grid over hot coals until the sides begin to turn. Turn over to brown other side as well. Serve with margarine.

Makes 15

*Muesli Bars***

90 g butter, softened
1/4 cup brown sugar
1/4 cup honey
2 tablespoons flour
1/2 cup pecan nuts or walnuts, chopped
1 cup rolled oats
1 tablespoon sunflower seeds
1/4 cup desiccated coconut
1/4 cup sultanas
3 dried apricots, chopped

Grease a 19 × 19 cm pan. Cream butter, sugar and honey in a small bowl until smooth. Stir in remaining ingredients and mix well. Press mixture over base of prepared pan and bake in a moderate oven for about 20 minutes or until lightly browned. Cool in pan before cutting into bars.

Nut Squares**

>1 egg, separated
>1/2 cup honey
>3 tablespoons wholewheat flour, sifted
>pinch salt
>1/2 cup nuts, chopped
>1/4 cup sesame seeds

Beat egg yolk until thick. Blend in honey. Combine with flour, salt, nuts and seeds. Fold in stiffly beaten egg white. Turn into oiled square pan and bake at 180 °C for 20–25 minutes until light brown. Cool and cut into squares.

P B Bars**

>1 1/2 cups peanut butter
>1 cup muesli
>1 cup dry milk powder
>1/2 cup brown sugar
>pinch salt
>1 cup toasted sesame seeds
>1/2 cup seedless raisins
>1/2 cup peanuts

Combine all ingredients. Add extra peanut butter if necessary to make the mixture stiff but not crumbly. Roll out to 1,25 cm thickness and cut into squares. Wrap individually in cling wrap.

Makes 60 small bars

*Peanut Brittle***

2 tablespoons butter
1½ cups sugar
½ cup syrup
½ cup water
1 cup unsalted peanuts
½ teaspoon bicarbonate of soda
1 teaspoon vanilla essence

Melt the butter in a saucepan and add the sugar, syrup and water. Stir until the sugar has dissolved and then boil without stirring. Boil until the mixture is quite brittle when tested in cold water. Add the soda, peanuts and vanilla and pour into a shallow buttered pan. Cool slightly and mark into squares. Break into pieces when cold.

Peanut Butter Bars

1 packet (200 g) wholemeal digestive biscuits
3 tablespoons margarine
3 tablespoons crunchy peanut butter

Crush the digestive biscuits and mix with the melted margarine. While still warm, stir in the peanut butter and make sure all ingredients are thoroughly blended. Turn into a lightly greased, shallow billy can and press down. Place in the fridge if prepared at home, or somewhere cool when on trail.* When set, cut into even-sized bars.

---

* Bars won't set in warm weather, so save this for winter hikes. Can also be used as a flan-top with fruit, custard, etc. for dessert.

*Peanut Butter Fudge***

*125–200 g crunchy peanut butter (depending on
   consistency/oiliness)
1/2 cup milk
3 cups sugar
1 tablespoon golden syrup
1 tablespoon butter
1 teaspoon vanilla essence*

Combine the peanut butter, milk, sugar and syrup in a saucepan. Boil gently, stirring constantly until a little of the mixture forms a soft ball when dropped into cold water. Remove from the heat, and add the butter and vanilla. Cool for a few minutes until tepid. Beat briskly until creamy. Pour into a shallow tin or dish and cut into squares when cool. (The fudge should be soft and sugary.)

*Peanut Butter and Granola Bars***

*1 1/2 cups Crunchy Granola
2 tablespoons powdered milk
2 tablespoons bran flakes
1/3 teaspoon cinnamon
pinch salt
1/4 cup raisins
1 teaspoon oil
2 tablespoons honey
1/2 teaspoon vanilla essence
1 1/2 teaspoons water
1/3 cup crunchy peanut butter
1 egg, well beaten*

Preheat oven to 120 °C. Generously grease and flour a baking pan and set aside. In a bowl, mix Crunchy Granola, milk powder, bran, cinnamon, salt and raisins. In a separate bowl, combine oil, honey, vanilla, water and peanut butter. Stir to mix well. Gradually stir Granola mixture into peanut butter mixture. Add egg and mix well. Press mixture into prepared baking pan and bake for 25 minutes. Allow to cool for 10–15 minutes in pan before cutting into bars.

Makes 32 bars

*Pear-lemon Squares***

>   1 cup plus 2 tablespoons flour
>   1/4 cup castor sugar
>   2 teaspoons grated lemon peel
>   1/4 cup butter or margarine
>   2 eggs
>   3/4 cup white sugar
>   3 tablespoons lemon juice
>   1 teaspoon baking powder
>   1/4 teaspoon salt
>   1 cup finely chopped dried pears

Preheat oven to 175 °C. Grease and flour a baking pan and set aside. In a bowl, combine 1 cup flour, castor sugar, 1 teaspoon grated lemon peel and butter or margarine. With a pastry blender or two knives, cut mixture until it resembles coarse cornmeal. Press mixture into bottom of prepared pan. Bake for 15 minutes, then remove from oven.

In a separate bowl, combine eggs and white sugar, beating until fluffy. Stir in lemon juice and remaining lemon peel. Add remaining 2 tablespoons flour, baking powder and salt. Mix well. Stir in dried pears. Pour mixture over partially baked layer and spread evenly to sides of pan. Bake for 20 minutes until top is bubbly and very lightly browned. Cool before cutting into squares. Lightly sprinkle with castor sugar.

Makes 36 squares

*Quick Fruit Bars***

    2 cups self-raising flour
    1½ cups light brown sugar
    1½ cups desiccated coconut
    250 g mixed fruitcake fruit
    ½ cup chopped pecan nuts
    2 eggs
    1 teaspoon vanilla essence
    125 g butter
    100 ml oil
    1 tablespoon cocoa powder
    2 teaspoons mixed ground spice

In a large bowl mix flour, sugar, coconut, fruit and nuts. Stir in eggs beaten with vanilla. Melt together the butter, oil, cocoa and ground spice over low heat. Add to flour mixture and mix well, then press firmly into an oiled 26 × 21 cm baking tin (the dough should be rather moist and slippery). Bake at 180 °C for 40 minutes or until firm. Cut into 24 jumbo bars or into 36 medium squares and leave to cool in tin.

Seed Biscuits**

> 80 g oats
> 40 g oat bran
> 300 g flour, sifted
> 480 g sugar
> pinch salt
> 260 g butter or margarine
> 50 ml golden syrup
> 50 ml water
> 7 ml bicarbonate of soda
> 60 g sesame seeds
> 15 g aniseed
> 30 g poppy seeds
> 75 g sunflower seeds

Combine oats, bran, flour, sugar and salt and set aside. In a small saucepan, melt butter, syrup and water over low heat. Remove from heat and stir in bicarb until mixture froths. Add to dry ingredients with seeds and stir well. Form mixture into small balls, place on a lightly greased baking tray, then flatten balls with a fork. Bake at 180 °C for 15–20 minutes or until evenly browned and cooked.

Makes about 80 biscuits

Sesame Confection**

> 1 cup sesame seeds
> 1/3 cup honey
> soy flour

Blend seeds and honey. Add enough flour to stiffen. Pat into oiled pan and chill. After a few days mixture will dry out and harden. Cut into squares.

Makes 9 squares

Sesame Seed Biscuits**

>250 g butter or margarine
>3/4 cup sugar
>3 teaspoons vanilla essence
>1 egg, beaten
>1/3 cup milk
>4 1/2 cups self-raising flour
>1 beaten egg yolk or 2 tablespoons milk for glazing
>1/4 cup sesame seeds

Cream together the butter, sugar and vanilla until smooth. Beat in the egg thoroughly, then add the milk. Stir in the flour and knead for a few seconds. Taking walnut-size pieces of dough, roll into long narrow strips 10 cm long and 1,25 cm wide. Twist each strip into a circle, coil or any other shape. Brush lightly with the beaten egg yolk or milk and sprinkle with sesame seeds.

Place the biscuits on a well-greased baking tray and bake at 180 °C until golden (approximately 20–25 minutes).

Makes 45 biscuits

Shortbread**

>2 3/4 cup flour
>pinch salt
>225 g margarine
>1/2 cup castor sugar

Sift flour and salt. Rub in margarine and add the sugar. Knead lightly to mix. Roll out the mixture and press lightly into a round 30 cm cake tin. Bake at 180 °C. Dredge with castor sugar. Cut into portions while still warm and leave to cool in tin.

SAVOURY NIBBLES

Biltong Fingers

Cut bread in fingers, spread with margarine and Marmite or Bovril and roll in grated biltong.

Herbed Wholewheat Straws**

>2⅔ cups wholewheat flour
>⅔ cup oil
>approx. 1 cup cold water
>3 tablespoons mixed herbs (rosemary, basil, marjoram, oregano, tarragon, etc.)

Blend all ingredients, adding enough water to make a stiff dough. Chill. Roll out on floured pastry board. Cut into strips and bake at 200 °C for about 10 minutes.

Makes 4–5 dozen straws

Nibbler's Treat**

>5 tablespoons butter or margarine
>5 teaspoons cooking oil
>2 cubes chicken stock, crumbled
>2 teaspoons curry powder
>½ teaspoon ground ginger
>½ teaspoon piri-piri
>3 cups Rice Krispies
>2 cups Post Toasties
>2 cups Cerix

Melt butter in cooking oil, add chicken stock cubes and mix. Add curry powder, ginger and piri-piri. Mix cereals. Add to butter mixture and mix well. Leave to cool.

*Sesame Seed Nibbles***

>1 cup wholewheat flour
>1/2 cup oil
>1/2 teaspoon salt
>approx. 2 tablespoons iced water
>1/2 cup sesame seeds

Blend flour and oil. Add salt and only enough water to make dough of piecrust consistency. Chill. Roll to 6 mm thickness. Cut into desired shapes. Arrange on oiled cooking sheet. Sprinkle with sesame seeds, pressing seeds lightly into dough. Bake at 180 °C for about 10 minutes until light brown.

*Wheat Germ Sticks***

>1 tablespoon honey
>1/2 cup oil
>1 1/4 cups milk
>2 cups wholewheat flour
>2 cups wheat germ
>1 teaspoon salt

Blend honey, oil and milk. Stir in remaining ingredients. Knead lightly. Roll out onto floured pastry board. Cut into sticks and bake at 160 °C for about 20 minutes or until light brown.

Makes 4–5 dozen sticks

SOUP AND DUMPLINGS

Cheese and Rice Soup*

1 onion, chopped
1 tablespoon margarine
1 tablespoon plain flour
1/4 teaspoon salt
1 teaspoon prepared mustard
1 cup water
1 cup skim milk (water and milk powder)
4 tablespoons cooked rice
2 tablespoons grated Cheddar cheese*

Sauté the onion in the margarine until tender. Add the flour, salt and mustard, then simmer for a further 2 minutes. Add the water and stir until it thickens. Simmer 10 minutes more. Add the milk and rice and bring to the boil. Remove from the heat, add the cheese, and stir until cheese has melted.

Serves 2

---

* Grate cheese at home.

Cream of Sweetcorn Soup

1 tablespoon margarine
1 tablespoon plain flour
½ cup chicken stock
200 g canned sweetcorn
salt and pepper to taste
1 sachet Worcestershire sauce (1 tablespoon)
¼ cup cream or evaporated milk
dried parsley

Melt margarine in saucepan. Stir in the flour and cook for a few minutes. Remove from the heat and gradually stir in the stock, seasoning and Worchestershire sauce. Bring gently to the boil and remove from the heat.

Strain the liquid off the corn and stir the corn into the pan. Bring back to the boil and simmer gently for 8 minutes. Stir the cream or milk into the soup and garnish with parsley.

Serves 2/3

Homemade Dry Soup Mix**

1 cup dry milk powder
1 cup nutritional yeast
1 cup soy flour
¼ cup dried herbs, mixed

Blend all ingredients. Store in tightly covered jar.

To make soup, use 3 tablespoons of this mix to each cup of water and boil together. If a food processor is available, dried peas and beans, barley, lentils or other dried legumes and cereals may also be ground to add to this soup mix.

Parsley Scone Dumplings*

50 g wholemeal flour
50 g oat flour
1½ teaspoons baking powder
2½ tablespoons margarine
1 tablespoon dried parsley
½ tablespoon black pepper
cold water to mix

Sieve wholemeal and oat flour and baking powder at home and add parsley and black pepper. On the trail, when ready to prepare, rub margarine into flour until mixture resembles breadcrumbs in consistency. Mix to a soft dough with cold water. Form into balls and add dumplings to soup to boil until done.

Makes 4 dumplings

SALADS

Bean Sprouts

Grow your own salad on the trail! Roll a handful of dried mung beans or alfalfa seeds in damp cheesecloth or a damp paper towel, and then wrap them in plastic. Store in your pack and rinse twice a day. Three days later you'll have crunchy sprouts to liven up your trail meals. Ways to serve sprouts: raw, as a separate dish; as a garnish for soups; blended into sandwich spreads; with meat, fish, eggs; in sauces; with Chinese noodles.

Rice and Green Pepper Salad

Mix cold cooked rice with some chopped green pepper and raw or fried onion. Toss in a dash of olive oil and a sachet of vinegar (1 tablespoon) or lemon and top with dried parsley.

Salad of India

1 banana, sliced
1/2 tablespoon chopped, unsalted nuts
1 tablespoon dates, pitted and chopped
1/2 teaspoon dried mint

Arrange banana on plate and garnish with other ingredients.

Serves 1

Tuna Salad

½ packet Spanish rice
1 tin tuna
1 green pepper
juice of small lemon
salt and black pepper

Boil rice until soft and allow to cool. Add all other ingredients and serve.

Serves 2–4

SAVOURY SAUCES

Easy Barbecue Sauce

> *1 sachet Worcestershire sauce (1 tablespoon)*
> *1 teaspoon paprika*
> *1 sachet tomato sauce (1 tablespoon)*
> *1 sachet mustard (1 tablespoon)*

Combine all ingredients and bring to the boil. Remove from heat and cool slightly.

Serves 1

Green Sauce for Pasta

> *¾ cup olive oil*
> *8 garlic cloves, crushed*
> *5 tablespoons dried parsley*
> *2 teaspoons black pepper*

Heat the olive oil in a small saucepan. When the oil is hot add the garlic and cook, stirring frequently, for 3 minutes or until the garlic begins to turn golden in colour. Add the parsley and pepper and simmer for a further 5 minutes. Serve with any pasta.

(It is recommended that this dish be shared amongst the group owing to the after-effects of garlic!)

PASTA

Bacon and Noodles*

> 250 g bacon (1 packet)
> 1 tablespoon margarine
> 1 onion, chopped
> 1 green pepper, pitted and chopped
> 1 clove garlic, crushed
> 1/2 teaspoon mixed dried herbs
> 1 cup noodles
> 1 l chicken stock (prepare from stock cubes)
> 1 cup grated Cheddar cheese*
> salt and pepper

Cut bacon into small pieces and fry in margarine with onion, green pepper, garlic and herbs. Cook noodles in stock until *al dente* and drain. Stir into bacon mixture and add cheese, salt and pepper.

Serves 4–5

---

* Grate cheese at home.

Chilli Fusilli*

500 g fusilli
boiling water
1 teaspoon salt
1 teaspoon oil or margarine

CHILLI AND TOMATO SAUCE:

2 tablespoons oil or margarine
1 small onion, chopped
1 teaspoon fresh or dried chilli, finely chopped
1 clove garlic, crushed
375 g Napolina chilli and tomato sauce
  (or packet sauce)
*4 tablespoons grated Mozzarella cheese**
Parmesan cheese to taste

Cook pasta in salted, boiling water with oil or margarine (to prevent sticking) for 10–12 minutes. Remove from heat and drain.

To make sauce, heat oil or margarine and sauté onion until tender. Add chillis, garlic and Napolina sauce. Simmer for a few minutes. Remove from heat and serve over pasta. Sprinkle with Mozzarella and then Parmesan cheese and serve immediately.

Serves 6

---

* Grate cheese at home.

Chinese Noodles with Napoli Sauce

> 1 packet Chinese noodles (i.e. Shogun)*
> 1 packet instant Knorr Napoli sauce
> Parmesan cheese

Boil water, add Chinese noodles and leave with lid closed for about 5 minutes. Drain. Prepare sauce and add to noodles. Serve sprinkled with Parmesan cheese.

Serves 2

* Use soup base in packet separately to make soup.

Curry Noodles

> 1 handful noodles
> ½ packet curry flavoured Toppers
> 10 soft, dried peaches
> 2½ cups water

Cut the dried peaches into small pieces. Put all the ingredients into a saucepan, bring to the boil and cook until done over low heat. (Could also be prepared according to the haybox cooking method.) Serve with chutney.

Serves 2

Funghi Fusilli

>   5 tablespoons oil or melted margarine
>   1 onion, finely chopped
>   2 teaspoons garlic flakes
>   1½ cups dried mushrooms
>   2 teaspoons dried parsley
>   10 slices salami, cut into strips
>   coarsely ground black pepper
>   salt to taste
>   500 g fusilli

Soak mushrooms and garlic until soft. Heat oil or margarine, add onion and garlic and sauté until golden. Add mushrooms and cook for 10 minutes. Add parsley, salami and seasoning, and toss well to heat through. Cook fusilli as directed on the packet. Pour sauce over pasta and toss well.

Makes 4 generous servings

Green Ribbon Pasta with Tuna Sauce

>   3 tablespoons olive oil
>   350 g tin tuna, drained and flaked
>   1 tablespoon dried parsley
>   1½ cups hot chicken stock (prepare from stock cube)
>   1 teaspoon black pepper
>   450 g green ribbon pasta

Cook and drain the pasta. Heat oil over moderate heat. Reduce heat to low when oil is hot and add the tuna and parsley. Cook, stirring constantly, for 5 minutes, then add the stock and black pepper. Continue cooking for a further 5 minutes, stirring frequently. Pour the sauce over the noodles and mix thoroughly.

Serves 4–6

Lasagne

1 packet Toppers, Bolognaise flavour
2 cups water
175 g lasagne sheets (4 sheets)*
1 packet instant white sauce
Parmesan or Cheddar cheese

Cook Toppers with water for 10 minutes. Grease pot and put two lasagne sheets in the bottom. Spoon over half of the Toppers mix. Put the other two lasagne sheets on the Toppers and finish with the rest of the Toppers. Prepare white sauce according to instructions on packet and pour over dish. Sprinkle Parmesan cheese over or put slices of Cheddar cheese on top. Cover pot for a few minutes to allow cheese to melt.

Serves 4

* Use the variety that doesn't need to be precooked.

Macaroni Cheese*

225 g macaroni
2 tablespoons margarine or oil
2 1/2 cups water
1 teaspoon salt
1 packet instant white sauce
1/2 teaspoon cayenne pepper
1/2 teaspoon prepared mustard
1 cup grated Cheddar cheese*

Cook the macaroni in the boiling, salted water with margarine or oil for about 10 minutes or until it is tender. Drain. In a separate pan, prepare the white sauce according to the instructions on the packet. Add the cayenne pepper, mustard and half of the cheese, mixing well. Add to the macaroni and stir well to blend. Sprinkle the remaining cheese over the macaroni mixture and put the lid on for a few minutes to allow the cheese to melt.

Serves 2–4

* Grate cheese at home

Noodles with Walnut Sauce*

> 55 g walnuts
> 2 teaspoons fresh parsley (or 1 teaspoon dried)
> 30 g fine wholemeal breadcrumbs
> salt and pepper to taste
> 3 tablespoons margarine
> 2 teaspoons oil
> 2 tablespoons creamy milk (use Cremora or full-cream milk powder)
> 1½ cups wholemeal noodles

At home, shell the walnuts and pound or grind them to make a paste. Add the finely chopped parsley, breadcrumbs and seasoning and mix well.

On trail, add to the above the margarine and oil and continue mixing until you have a thick, creamy sauce. Stir in the milk and adjust the seasoning. (If the sauce is too thick, add more milk.) Cook the noodles in salted, boiling water until tender, drain and mix with the walnut sauce.

Serves 2–4

*Prawn Pasta**

>1 cup pasta shells
>packet instant parsley sauce
>150 g tinned prawns, drained
>salt and black pepper to taste
>1/4 cup grated Cheddar cheese*

Cook and drain the pasta. Prepare the sauce according to the instructions on the packet and pour over the shells. Stir in the prawns and seasoning and mix together well. Sprinkle with cheese and heat through.

Serves 2

* Grate cheese at home.

*Red Beans and Pasta**

>1 cup red beans
>1 1/2 cups small pasta shapes
>3 tablespoons olive oil
>1 fresh onion, thinly sliced
>1 garlic clove, finely chopped
>450 g tinned tomatoes, chopped
>2 teaspoons dried basil
>2 teaspoons dried parsley
>3/4 cup grated Gruyère or Cheddar cheese*

Soak and cook the beans. Boil the pasta in lightly salted water for about 10 minutes until tender. Drain and rinse. While the pasta is cooking, heat the oil in a saucepan on low heat. Sauté onions and garlic until soft. Add the tomatoes and herbs and cook gently, uncovered, for 3 minutes. Mix in the beans and pasta and heat through. Scatter cheese over the top.

Serves 4–6

* Grate cheese at home.

Spaghetti Bolognaise

1 packet 120 g Toppers, Bolognaise flavour
1½ cups spaghetti (break into small pieces)
2 cloves garlic, crushed
coarsely ground black pepper
dash each of sage and thyme

Mix all the ingredients together and cook according to the haybox cooking method (see page 22). Serve with Parmesan cheese and a fresh tomato, if possible.

Serves 4

Summer Party Pasta

1½ cups shell noodles
1½ cups penne noodles
1 teaspoon salt
1 teaspoon oil or margarine
1 teaspoon dried thyme

MUSHROOM AND TOMATO SAUCE:

2 tablespoons oil or margarine
1 packet instant mushroom and tomato sauce, prepared
½ cup dried mushrooms*
salt and black pepper
1 small tin boiled mussels (optional)

Cook pasta in lightly salted, boiling water with oil or margarine for about 15 minutes. Drain. Toss with thyme.

To make sauce, heat oil or margarine in pan, add prepared sauce and mushrooms and simmer for few minutes. Remove from heat, and add pasta, mussels, salt and pepper to taste.

Serves 6–8

* Soak thoroughly before adding to sauce.

Tagliatelle with Salami and Cheese*

>1 1/2 cups wholewheat tagliatelle
>4 tablespoons olive oil
>1 fresh onion, thinly sliced
>1 clove garlic, finely chopped
>about 20 slices peppercorn-coated salami, cut into strips
>350 g tin tomatoes, chopped
>2 teaspoons dried parsley
>2 tablespoons grated Gruyère cheese*
>Parmesan cheese to taste

Cook the tagliatelle in lightly salted boiling water for about 12 minutes or until tender. Drain and keep warm.

Heat the oil in a pan over low heat. Put in the onion, garlic and salami and cook until the onion is soft. Mix in the tagliatelle, tomatoes, Parmesan cheese and parsley and cook for a minute so the tomatoes just heat through. Scatter Gruyère cheese over the top and cover for 2 minutes to allow cheese to melt.

Serves 4–6

* Grate cheese at home.

Tortellini in Cream

>1 packet (250 g) tortellini
>1 teaspoon salt
>1/3 cup Parmesan cheese
>100 g tin cream
>dried herbs to taste

Cook tortellini until done in salted water. Drain and toss lightly with cream, cheese and herbs.

Serves 2–4

Trail Spaghetti Dinner

>1½ l water
>27 g packet tomato soup
>32 g packet spaghetti sauce mix
>1 cup biltong or soya mince
>1 cup noodles
>Parmesan cheese

Bring water to the boil. Add soup powder, sauce mix and meat. Cook until tender. Add noodles or cook separately. Serve with Parmesan cheese.

Serves 4

Tuna Curry Noodles

>1 cup noodles
>2 tablespoons margarine
>2 tablespoons flour
>1 tablespoon curry powder
>salt and black pepper
>1½ cups milk
>1 apple, chopped
>½ cup raisins
>¼ cup cashew nuts (optional)
>200 g can tuna, drained and flaked

Cook and drain noodles. In a saucepan, melt margarine. Remove from heat and stir in flour, curry powder and seasoning. Gradually add half the milk. Return to stove and cook for a few minutes. Add remaining milk and cook until sauce boils and thickens. Stir in apple, raisins, nuts and tuna. Heat through. Pour over noodles and serve with chutney and desiccated coconut.

Serves 4

Tuna Spirals

>1 cup pasta spirals
>2 cups boiling water
>1/2 onion, finely chopped
>1 tablespoon oil or melted margarine
>200 g can tomatoes, chopped
>90 g tin tuna in brine, drained
>1 teaspoon dried mixed herbs

Cook pasta in boiling salted water until tender. Drain. Sauté onion in oil or margarine, add tomatoes, tuna and herbs and fry for a few minutes. Serve over pasta.

Serves 2

Warm Spaghetti Salad

>500 g spaghetti
>1 teaspoon salt
>1 teaspoon oil or margarine
>
>SAUCE:
>
>2 tablespoons oil or margarine
>1 small onion, chopped
>1 small green pepper, seeded and chopped
>2 cloves garlic, crushed
>375 g Napolina Bolognaise sauce*
>1 teaspoon dried oregano

Boil spaghetti in salted water with oil or margarine. Drain.

Heat oil or margarine and sauté onion. Add green pepper, garlic and sauce. Simmer for 10 minutes. Add oregano and toss with pasta.

Serves 6

---

* Or substitute with a light-weight instant packet sauce.

VEGETABLES

Asparagus

Heat a small can of asparagus, drain and serve with melted margarine and nutmeg.

Cabbage in Cheese Sauce

Serve rehydrated dried cabbage in an instant cheese sauce (or see under Cheesy Baked Potatoes on page 92 for homemade cheese sauce).

Carrots and Potatoes

Cover half a packet of dried carrots, half a packet of dried potatoes and a few dried onions with sufficient water to cover vegetables. Cook according to haybox method (see page 22). When tender (approximately 1½ hours), add a little margarine and salt and lightly mash vegetables with a fork.

Carrots in White Sauce

Prepare dried carrots according to instructions on packet or cook according to haybox method (see page 22). Serve with an instant white sauce.

Cheesy Baked Potatoes*

Wrap potatoes at home in heavy tin foil. On trail, cook the potatoes by putting them in hot coals until done. Open the foil, cut a square on top of the potatoes and squeeze until the flesh pops out. Top with cheese sauce:

> 1 tablespoon margarine
> 1 tablespoon flour
> 1/2 cup milk (water and milk powder)
> salt to taste
> 3 tablespoons Melrose cheese spread

Place margarine, flour, milk and salt into a pan over medium heat. Stir in cheese spread until smooth, then spoon over baked potatoes.

Note: This sauce can be used over any vegetable of your choice.

Green Beans in Mushroom Sauce

Serve rehydrated green beans in an instant cream of mushroom sauce. Sprinkle with almonds.

Mint-glazed Carrots with Peas

Mix half a packet of dried carrots with a quarter of a packet of dried peas and then cook according to the haybox method (see page 22). When cooked, add a little salt, a tablespoon of margarine and 1/4 cup sugar. Cook over medium heat until sauce has reduced. Add 1 teaspoon of dried mint just before serving.

Mushrooms

Soak dried mushrooms until tender, or prepare them according to the haybox cooking method. Drain. In a pan fry 2 tablespoons of margarine, 2 crushed garlic cloves, salt and black pepper. Add mushrooms. If you are prepared to carry a small lemon, a few drops of juice will add special flavour to this dish.

Potato Nests

Prepare potatoes as for Cheesy baked potatoes (see page 92). Make a hollow nest in each potato and fill with mashed banana and chutney. (Carry banana in billycan to avoid it getting squashed.)

Rice Patties

> 1 cup cooked brown rice
> 1 cup fresh or dried sweet potatoes, cooked and mashed
> 1 tablespoon melted margarine
> 1 tablespoon nutritional yeast
> $1/8$ teaspoon mace
> milk powder

Combine all ingredients and bind with as much dry milk powder as mixture will hold. Shape into patties and arrange in oiled pan. Broil each side until browned.

Risotto*

>2 tablespoons oil
>1 onion, chopped
>1 clove garlic, crushed
>1 cup raw brown rice
>3 tablespoons nutritional yeast
>1/2 teaspoon dried rosemary
>1/2 teaspoon dried parsley
>1/2 teaspoon ground turmeric
>2 cups chicken stock (use stock cubes)
>1/2 cup grated Cheddar cheese*

Heat oil and sauté onion and garlic. Add rice and cook for 3 minutes. stirring constantly. Dissolve yeast, herbs and turmeric in stock. Pour 1/2 cup of stock into rice mixture, cover and simmer gently, gradually adding rest of stock as liquid is absorbed. Rice should be tender in about 30 minutes. Add 1/4 cup cheese a few minutes before rice is done. When cheese is melted through, remove from heat. Top with remaining cheese and serve.

Serves 6

* Grate cheese at home.

Sautéed Sprouts

>2 tablespoons oil
>1 cup sprouts
>stock to cover

Sauté sprouts briefly in oil. Add stock. Cover pan and cook over low heat for 3 minutes. If desired, add any of the following while cooking: herbs, onions, carrots or mushrooms (if you are using dried products, soak them first).

Stewed Cabbage

Prepare ½ packet dried cabbage, ¼ packet dried potatoes and 1 tablespoon dried onions (or a small, fresh onion) according to the haybox method (see page 22). When done, add salt and a tablespoon of margarine and mash vegetables with a fork.

Sweet Potatoes

Prepare a packet of dried sweet potatoes according to the haybox cooking method (see page 22) together with the following: 1 stick cinnamon, dried naartjie peel, 4 tablespoons brown sugar, 1 tablespoon margarine and a pinch of salt.

Sweet Potatoes in Foil

Wrap washed sweet potatoes in heavy-duty aluminium foil and put in the coals until soft. Open foil, slit the potatoes in the middle and serve with a little margarine. For a tasty variation, put a marshmallow in the slit and close the foil again until the marshmallow has melted.

Sweet Potatoes with Marshmallows

Prepare a packet of dried sweet potatoes according to the haybox cooking method (see page 22). When soft (about 1½ hours later) add the following: ½ cup milk (dissolved milk powder), 6 marshmallows cut in half, ½ teaspoon salt and 1 teaspoon sugar. Simmer slowly, stirring constantly until milk has reduced and marshmallows have melted.

Tasty Instant Potatoes

Prepare potatoes according to the instructions on the pack. Make sure you have added enough boiling water, as the secret of successful instant potatoes is a soft, smooth consistency. Add salt, black pepper, dried parsley and a little margarine and mix until creamy.

OTHER MAIN MEALS

Baked Potatoes with Shrimps or Mussels*

Large potatoes
tinned shrimps or mussels
salt and black pepper
vinegar

Wrap potatoes in heavy-duty foil at home. On trail, put potatoes in hot coals until done. Unwrap and cut potatoes in half. Top with shrimps or mussels and season with salt, pepper and vinegar.

Biltong Potjie*

½ packet Spanish rice
*handful grated Cheddar cheese**
handful sliced biltong
sachet vinegar (1 tablespoon)

Cook rice until done, add other ingredients and mix until cheese has melted.

Serves 1–2

---

* Grate cheese at home.

Cheese Fondue*

Buy a packet of pre-packed cheese fondue or prepare your own: Grate Gruyère cheese* and mix with maizena (about 2 tablespoons maizena to 1½ cups cheese), and a little kirsch. Heat until cheese melts. Tear chunks off bread and dip into cheese with a fork. Also delicious with tinned sausages and fresh bananas.

* Do this at home.

Chicken à La King

>   37 g Maggi Fix 'à la king' flavour
>   2 cups water
>   9 teaspoons Cremora
>   105 g tin smoked mussels
>   105 g Tastic Savoury Classics rice, chicken almondine
>   flavour

Prepare sauce according to instruction on packet, substituting water and Cremora for fresh milk. When cooked, add mussels and stir through. Prepare rice according to instructions on packet and serve with sauce.

Serves 2–4

Cooked-in-the-pan Pizza Margherita*

FOR BASE:
170 g plain wholemeal flour
1 teaspoon baking powder
salt to taste
water to mix (approx 1/2 cup)

FOR TOPPING:
1 small tin tomatoes, chopped
1 cup grated cheese
1 teaspoon dried oregano
2 teaspoons oil or margarine
salt and black pepper to taste

At home, mix together the flour, baking powder and salt. Grate cheese.

On trail, add water gradually to above mixture, kneading to make a dough. Continue kneading until dough is smooth and soft then divide into two and roll out into thin rounds. (Use an empty film cannister or clean gas cannister as a roller.) Pour a little oil into a pan and heat until hot but not smoking. Turn down heat and cook dough slowly for two minutes.

Turn the pizza and cover with half of the tomatoes, then half of the cheese. Sprinkle with herbs and season well. Continue cooking for a few minutes to brown the underside of the pizza and heat the topping.

Cook the second pizza in the same way.

Let your imagination run riot with additional toppings: anchovies, salami, pepperoni sausage, etc.

Makes 2 pizzas

Curried Salmon

1 tablespoon margarine
1 small onion, chopped
2 teaspoons curry powder
2 teaspoons flour
1/2 cup chicken stock
1 sachet chutney (1 tablespoon)
1 sachet vinegar (1 tablespoon)
175 g can salmon

Melt the margarine, add the onion and fry until golden. Stir in the curry powder, cook for about 3 minutes, then add the flour and continue cooking for another 2 minutes. Remove from heat, pour in the stock gradually, stirring constantly. Return to heat and bring to the boil. Reduce heat and add vinegar and chutney. Allow to simmer for 10 minutes. Add the salmon to the sauce and heat through but do not allow to boil or break up the fish. Serve with rice.

Serves 2

Hamburger Patties

120 g Toppers, curry flavour
1 cup oats
1 teaspoon margarine
4 sachets mustard (4 tablespoons)
4 sachets chutney (4 tablespoons)

Prepare Toppers according to instruction on packet, but use only 2 cups of water. When done, add oats and stir for a few minutes. Set aside to allow oats to bind with Toppers. Mixture should be rather stiff. As soon as mixture is cool enough to handle, press into patties and fry on each side in melted margarine until brown. Be careful not to break patties when turning them.

Serve between breadrolls with mustard or chutney, or on Smash.

Makes 8 patties

Kipper Pie

>200 g John West kipper fillets in vegetable oil
>30 g Cadbury Smash instant potatoes
>salt and black pepper
>1 teaspoon margarine

Heat kippers in can (see instructions on can). Add enough boiling water to Smash to form soft mash. Add salt and black pepper to taste and stir in margarine. Spoon mash on top of kippers and serve with small tin of baked beans or peas or dehydrated vegetables.

Serves 2

Lentil Curry

>2 cups lentils
>1 onion, chopped
>2 tablespoons margarine, melted
>1 clove garlic, finely chopped
>1 teaspoon turmeric
>1 teaspoon curry powder
>small piece of cinnamon
>small piece of fresh ginger, chopped
>1/2 teaspoon salt
>1 teaspoon sugar
>1 sachet vinegar (1 tablespoon)

Cook the lentils according to the haybox cooking method. Sauté the onion in margarine until tender. Add the garlic and sauté for another minute. Mix the spices, salt, sugar and vinegar and add to the onion and garlic. Sauté for another 3 minutes. Add the lentils and ¼ cup water and simmer for 15 minutes. Serve with rice and chutney.

Serves 2

Malay Bobotie

>1 cup rice
>100 g Moir's Meat Magic, oriental flavour
>120 g Toppers, savoury flavour

Boil rice until done and put aside. Cook Toppers and Meat Magic together with 3 cups water and cook over very low heat (or use haybox cooking method) until done. Serve with Wellington's Cape Malay stewed peaches and rice.

Serves 6

Meal-in-one*

>2 l water
>2 teaspoons salt
>2 cups mealiemeal
>250 g biltong, sliced or grated*
>grated cheese*

Bring water to the boil and add salt and mealiemeal. Cook until done. Add biltong and mix well. Sprinkle with cheese.

Serves 6

* Grate cheese and biltong at home.

Savoury Mince

120 g Toppers, savoury flavour
1 beef stock cube
2 teaspoons curry powder
2 teaspoons garlic flakes (or 2 fresh cloves)
27 g packet vegetable soup
2 tablespoons sugar
4 tablespoons raisins
1 bayleaf
1/4 teaspoon nutmeg
1/4 teaspoon ginger
1/4 teaspoon ground cinnamon
1 cup rice

Bring 1,5 *l* water to the boil and add all ingredients, including the rice. Simmer for 30–40 minutes or until cooked.

Serves 6–8

Shepherd's Pie

5 tablespoons margarine
1 small onion, finely chopped
120 g Toppers
1 teaspoon dried herbs
1 sachet Worcestershire sauce (1 tablespoon)
30 g Cadbury Smash instant potato
1/2 teaspoon salt
1/2 teaspoon black pepper

Cook Toppers according to the instructions on the packet. Melt 3 tablespoons margarine, add onion and fry until golden. Stir in the prepared Toppers, herbs and Worcestershire sauce and cook for 3 minutes, stirring constantly.

Prepare Smash according to the instructions on the packet. Add salt, black pepper and 2 tablespoons margarine to Smash and spoon over Toppers mix. Using a fork, draw decorative lines over the potatoes. Serve with a small tin of peas (or prepare dehydrated peas), sweetened with a teaspoon of sugar.

Serves 6

Spiced Black-eyed Beans

1 cup black-eyed beans
4 tablespoons margarine
1 onion, thinly sliced
1 clove garlic, finely chopped
1 tablespoon ground mixed spice
1 tablespoon paprika
½ cup chicken stock
2 tablespoons tomato purée
2 tablespoons dried parsley

Soak the beans and cook according to the haybox cooking method (see page 22). Heat the margarine in a pan on low heat. Add the onion, garlic, mixed spice and paprika and cook until the onion is soft. Stir in the beans, stock, tomato purée and parsley. Cover and keep on a very low heat for 10 minutes.

Serve with brown rice.

Serves 2–4

Trail Casserole

>1 packet mixed dried vegetables
>1 teaspoon dried herbs
>salt and pepper
>340 g tin corned beef

Prepare vegetables according to the haybox cooking method (see page 22) until done. Add herbs, seasoning and beef and cook slowly over low heat for 5–10 minutes. Serve with rice or Smash.

Serves 3–4

Vegetarian Bobotie*

>1 tablespoon margarine
>2 chopped onions
>2 cups finely chopped nuts*
>1 tablespoon curry powder
>1 cup breadcrumbs
>2 teaspoons apricot jam
>1 teaspoon turmeric
>2 tablespoons seedless raisins
>1 sachet chutney (1 tablespoon)
>1 tablespoon vinegar or lemon juice
>1 egg, beaten (a hassle to carry, but worth it)
>1/2 teaspoon desiccated coconut
>salt to taste
>1 teaspoon Marmite, dissolved in 1 cup hot water

CUSTARD TOPPING:

>1 egg
>3/4 cup milk (water and full-cream milk powder)
>salt and pepper
>4 bay or lemon leaves

Fry onions lightly in the margarine. Remove from heat and add the rest of the ingredients, except the hot water and Marmite. When mixed, gradually stir in the hot water and Marmite.

Prepare the topping by beating the egg, milk and seasoning together with a fork. Pour over the nut mixture and insert the bay or lemon leaves into bobotie. Cover and set over low heat, taking care not to burn the dish. When thoroughly heated cook for an hour according to the haybox cooking method (see page 22).

Serve with rice and the usual curry accompaniments.

Serves 6

---

* Put them through the blender at home.

DESSERTS

Apple and Date Charlotte

    6 slices bread
    margarine
    4 apples (soaked, dried apples can also be used)
    2 or 3 tablespoons white sugar
    1 cup chopped dates
    cinnamon
    brown sugar

Spread the bread with the margarine, removing the crusts if preferred. Cut the slices of bread into fingers or cubes. Simmer the peeled apple in the minimum of water, adding the white sugar. When soft, add the dates and a sprinkling of cinnamon. Sprinkle the bottom of a pot with a little brown sugar. Put half the bread in the pan with the buttered side towards the sugar so it will brown and crisp. Cover with the apple mixture, then the rest of the bread, this time with the buttered side uppermost. Sprinkle lightly with brown sugar. Set over low heat until warmed through.

Serves 6–8

Baked Stuffed Apples*

    1 teaspoon brown sugar
    1 teaspoon chopped raisins
    1 teaspoon chopped hazelnuts or walnuts
    pinch lemon rind, finely grated*
    pinch ground cinnamon
    rum or sherry
    margarine

Cut squares of foil for each apple and grease the inside of each square with margarine. Rinse, dry and core apples. Stuff cavities with a mixture of the brown sugar, raisins, hazelnuts or walnuts, lemon rind and cinnamon. Pour a teaspoon of rum or sherry over each cavity and dot with margarine. Wrap each stuffed apple in its buttered foil. Stand them on a grid over hot coals and bake until soft (approx. 30 minutes).

* Grate the lemon rind at home.

Caramelled Apples

> 1/2 cup white sugar
> 1/2 cup water
> 4 dessert apples

For the caramel sauce, put the sugar and 4 tablespoons of water into a pan, stir until the sugar has dissolved, then boil without stirring until golden brown. Add the rest of the water and blend with the caramel. Peel, core and slice the apples, put onto a plate, add the warm caramel and allow to cool. Turn over once or twice so the apples absorb the sauce.

Serves 4

Caramel Popcorn

> 1/4 cup unpopped corn
>
> SAUCE:
>
> 3 tablespoons golden syrup
> 1/2 cup castor sugar
> 1 1/2 teaspoons vinegar
> 3 tablespoons margarine
> 1 tablespoon desiccated coconut

Melt a little margarine in a pan, add corn, cover and pop corn on high heat. Take care not to burn popcorn.

In a separate pan, combine syrup, sugar and vinegar and heat until deep golden brown. Stir in the margarine, popped corn and coconut. Press into a lightly greased pan. When cold, break into pieces.

Caramel Sauce

>   1 cup sugar
>   1 tablespoon margarine
>   2/3 cup cold water
>   1/4 cup boiling water
>   3/4 cup warm milk*
>   1 teaspoon cornflour
>   1 teaspoon salt
>   1 teaspoon vanilla essence

Heat the sugar, margarine and cold water in a pan, stirring until the syrup is clear and light brown in colour. Add the boiling water and stir until smooth. Add the milk. Mix the cornflour and salt to a paste with a little cold milk and stir this in slowly. Boil for 3 minutes, remove from heat and add vanilla.

Serve hot with fruit, over Marie biscuits or with marshmallows.

* Mix full-cream milk powder with water and heat.

Cardinal Peaches

>   2 tablespoons red currant jelly
>   2 tablespoons white sugar
>   1 cup water
>   4 firm but ripe peaches*

Put the red currant jelly, sugar and water into a pan. Heat until the jelly melts. Skin and halve the peaches (if using fresh ones), put into the syrup and simmer gently for 5 minutes.

Serves 4

* Can be substituted by tinned peaches or soaked, dried peaches.

Chocolate Fondue I

>*100 g slab milk chocolate*
>*410 g can sweetened full-cream condensed milk*
>*kirsch*

Break the chocolate into squares and place all ingredients in cooking pot over low heat. Stir until chocolate has melted and ingredients have combined. Serve with fresh or dried fruit, marshmallows or finger biscuits.

Chocolate Fondue II

>*100 g slab Albany chocolate*
>*310 g tin cream*
>*2 tablespoons Sabre or Cointreau liqueur*

Break chocolate into pot and add cream. Place over low heat until chocolate has melted. Add liqueur and stir. Serve with marshmallows, fresh or dried fruit or finger biscuits.

Chocolate-stuffed Bananas

4 large bananas*
100 g slab milk chocolate
rum, coffee liqueur or brandy (optional)

Cut away a thin section of skin down the length of the banana. Break the chocolate into squares and halve the squares. Press the chocolate into the banana flesh and braai the bananas, uncovered, until the flesh starts to soften and the chocolate melts (about 10 minutes). Pour a little liqueur or brandy over and serve.

* Pack in billycans and eat on first day.

Cornflake Flan

4 tablespoons margarine
4 tablespoons castor sugar
2 teaspoons golden syrup or honey
2¼ cups cornflakes, slightly crushed
canned fruit

Cream the margarine, sugar and syrup or honey. Add the cornflakes. Form into a flan shape in a pan or tin plate. Set in a cool place and fill with fruit or date filling (see page 112).

Custard

>1 1/2 cups water
>5 heaped tablespoons Cremora
>3 heaped tablespoons custard powder
>4 teaspoons sugar
>pinch salt

Boil water and stir in Cremora. Mix custard powder with a little cold water and add to boiling water and Cremora. Add sugar and salt and cook on low heat for a few minutes.

Date Filling for Flan*

>1 1/2 cups finely chopped dates
>1/2 cup water
>1/2 cup sugar
>1 teaspoon lemon juice
>1/2 teaspoon grated lemon rind*
>1/3 cup chopped pecan nuts

Combine dates, water and sugar in a pan and cook over low heat until thickened (20–25 minutes), stirring frequently. When thickened, add lemon juice, lemon rind and nuts. Cool and fill flan (see cornflake flan, page 111)

* Grate lemon rind at home.

Fried Apple Rings

>dried apple rings
>margarine
>sugar
>cinnamon

Soak apple rings in enough hot water to cover for about 20 minutes. Heat margarine in a pot, add apples and cook covered over low heat for 15 minutes. Mix sugar and cinnamon (one teaspoon cinnamon to half-a-cup of sugar) and sprinkle over apples. Cook uncovered for a further 15–20 minutes, basting occasionally with the juice in the saucepan. Serve hot.

Honey and Almond Fondue

250 g Nestlé Easy Melt Chocolate
½ cup (125 ml tin) cream
½ cup honey
½ cup chopped almonds

Break chocolate into pot with cream and honey. Heat over slow heat until chocolate has melted, then stir in almonds. Serve with dried fruit.

Mock Cream Sauce

4 tablespoons margarine
¾ cup castor sugar
2 tablespoons warm milk*
1 teaspoon vanilla essence

Beat the margarine to a creamy consistency with a fork, slowly adding the sugar. Add the milk and vanilla essence drop by drop, beating continuously. (Do not add milk and vanilla too quickly, or sauce will curdle.) Serve with pears in red wine (page 115) or any other dessert.

---

* Mix full-cream milk powder with water and heat.

Noodle and Prune Bake

450 g pitted prunes
175 g wide noodles
1/4 cup margarine
1/2 cup sugar
1 tablespoon ground cinnamon

Stew the prunes and reserve 2/3 cup of the liquid. Cook the noodles in unsalted water and drain.

Using 2 teaspoons of the margarine, grease a deep saucepan. Lay one-third of the noodles in the pan and dot with a quarter of the remaining margarine and half of the prunes. Combine the sugar and cinnamon and sprinkle half of this mixture over the prunes. Continue making layers this way, ending with a layer of noodles. Pour the reserved prune juice over the mixture and dot with the remaining margarine.

Place the pan on low heat, being careful not to burn the dish. As soon as it is warmed through, and without lifting the lid of the saucepan, put the saucepan into a sleeping bag and cook according to the instructions for haybox cooking (see page 22) for a further 30 minutes.

Serves 6

Orange Cream

3 oranges
410 g can creamed rice
3 tablespoons marmalade, jam or red currant jelly

Peel the oranges and slice the fruit neatly. Blend some of the fruit with the rice. Spoon into 4 individual plates (or mugs). Heat the marmalade, jam or jelly. Arrange the rest of the oranges on the rice and top with the hot preserve.

Serves 4

Oranges in Foil

>4 oranges
>1/5 cup rum
>1/4 cup brown sugar

Peel the oranges and cut a cross on top of each. Pour in rum and brown sugar, wrap in heavy-duty aluminium foil and put on medium coals until soft. Serve with marshmallows.

Serves 4

Pears in Red Wine

>1 can pears
>red wine (buy those in light alloy cans)
>small tin cream (or mock cream sauce, page 113)
>1 teaspoon ground cinnamon
>sugar (optional)

Drain the pears and cook over low heat for 10 minutes in enough red wine to cover. Put pears in serving bowls and add cream and a little sugar, if required, to wine in pan. Heat through and pour over pears. Sprinkle with cinnamon.

Serves 6

Prune Stew

Simmer dried prunes for 30 minutes in water and sugar. Add allspice, cloves, cinnamon, lemon, nutmeg, and sherry for a tasty dessert.

Simple Baked Apples

1 apple per person
2 teaspoons sugar, honey or syrup

Rinse apples and dry them thoroughly. Pluck out their stems. Wrap each apple tightly in a square of heavy-duty foil (or a double thickness of light foil). While the main course is being eaten, set foil-wrapped apples on the glowing coals. After about 10 minutes turn them over and cook for 10–15 minutes longer on the other side. Serve hot with sugar, honey or syrup.

Spiced Apples with Honey

dried apple rings, soaked
2 tablespoons margarine, melted
3 tablespoons honey
1/2 teaspoon ground mixed spice

Brush apples with melted margarine and lay them in a flat, heatproof plate or pan, overlapping as little as possible, with the margarine-side under. Pour honey and spice over apples and put on high gas flame or coals. Turn often until apples are brown and bubbling.

Trifle

½ packet finger biscuits
225 g tin fruit cocktail
2 teaspoons sherry
1 cup (250 ml) Ultramel custard, warmed*

Cut or break the biscuits into small pieces in individual plates (or mugs). Moisten with a little fruit juice and sherry, then top with fruit. Spoon the warm custard over the top and allow to cool.

Serves 4

* Alternatively, make your own custard (see page 112)

DRINKS

Banana Milk Shake

> 1 banana, mashed
> 1 cup milk (water and full-cream milk powder)
> 1 teaspoon honey

Mix ingredients in a shaker, if available, or any container with a tight lid and shake for a few minutes. Serve either hot or cold.

Serves 1

Brown Russian

> 50 g plain chocolate
> 1 cup milk (water and full-cream milk powder)
> 1 tablespoon vodka

Heat the milk gently, then pour three-quarters of it into a mug. Add the chocolate to the remaining milk and melt over a low heat until thoroughly blended. Return the rest of the milk to the pan, remove from the heat and stir. Pour the drink into a mug, stir in the vodka and serve.

Serves 1

Chocolate Soldier

> 1 part Eine Kleine Nachtmusik liqueur
> 4 parts hot milk (water and full-cream milk powder)
> 1 stick cinnamon

Mix the liqueur and milk in a mug and stir with the cinnamon. Sprinkle a little nutmeg over if available.

Serves 1

Cocoa

For warmth at night, prepack cocoa in portions, allowing 2 tablespoons cocoa to 7 teaspoons sugar and 5 tablespoons milk powder. Add boiling water.

Serves 2

Ginger Tea

> 1 tablespoon tea leaves
> 2 thin slices fresh ginger root
> 1 cup boiling water
> sugar (optional)

Pour the boiling water over the tea leaves and ginger and infuse for 3–5 minutes. Pour into a heated cup and serve with or without sugar to taste.

Serves 1

Harry's Cape Velvet

> 410 ml tin Ideal milk
> 410 ml tin condensed milk
> 2 heaped teaspoons coffee, stirred into a little bit of hot water
> 1 cup brandy or whisky

Mix together and put into a plastic bottle for a delightful trail sundowner. Can also be poured over Nuttikrust biscuits for dessert.

Hot Punch

> 1 l red wine (buy those sold in light alloy cans)
> 1 orange, cut into quarters*
> 2 dried figs, cut into quarters
> 5 chopped almonds
> 3 whole cloves
> 2 sticks cinnamon
> 1 tablespoon sugar
> brandy, curaçao or kirsch

Pour wine over solid ingredients and place over slow heat. Stir until all the sugar has completely dissolved, then raise the heat and bring the mixture to the boil. Lower the heat and simmer for about 10 minutes.

Remove the pan from the heat, cover and leave the mixture to infuse for a further 5 minutes. With a spoon, remove all the solids from the wine. Return the wine to the heat and add a little brandy, curaçao or kirsch. Reheat until liquid begins to bubble, but do not allow it to boil. Pour into mugs and, if you like, garnish with thin slices of orange rind.

Serves 4–6

* You may prefer to use the rind only.

Hot Semolina Drink

>2 cups milk (water and full-cream milk powder)
>1 tablespoon semolina
>sugar to taste
>ground cinnamon

Place the milk, semolina and sugar to taste in a pan over low heat and cook gently for 10 minutes, stirring. Serve in mugs and sprinkle cinnamon on top.

Hot Spiced Orange Juice

>1 small box Ceres orange juice
>1 small cinnamon stick
>a little grated nutmeg

This is not only refreshing, but also warming and healthy. Heat the orange juice with the stick of cinnamon. Pour into a mug, top with nutmeg and add the cinnamon stick for decoration.

Serves 1

Mozart Coffee

For a special treat, add a little Eine Kleine Nachtmusik liqueur to black coffee. Divide a small tin of cream between the mugs.

Peanut Milk

>   4 tablespoons smooth peanut butter
>   1 l water
>   1/2 teaspoon salt
>   sugar (optional)

Put the peanut butter into a pan and add the water very gradually, stirring steadily, until the two are thoroughly blended. Bring the mixture to the boil and cook over medium heat for 10 minutes, stirring occasionally. Add salt (and sugar if desired). Beat with a fork just before serving. Serve hot or cold.

Serves 4–5

The author welcomes comments and critism, and would appreciate the receipt of new recipes for inclusion in a subsequent edition of this book.

Please send to: Rita van Dyk
P O Box 23874
Innesdale
0031

Notes

Notes

Notes

Notes

Notes